paper books

Accents

an anthology of poetry from the English-speaking world

Michael Chapman and Tony Voss

AD. DONKER / PUBLISHER

AD. DONKER (PTY) LTD
A subsidiary of Donker Holdings (Pty) Ltd
P O Box 41021
Craighall
2024

First published 1986

ISBN 0 86852 063 2

Typeset by M.M. Fourie, Johannesburg
Printed and bound by Creda Press (Pty) Ltd., Cape Town

CONTENTS

FOREWORD

This selection is aimed at two readerships: at first-year university, college and technikon students particularly in South Africa; more generally at those who wish to acquaint themselves with, and enjoy, the astonishing range of poetry in English from the Middle Ages to the present day. The English inheritance is traced through, among others, Chaucer, Shakespeare, Milton, Pope, Wordsworth, Tennyson and Yeats, while the heterogeneity of English-language poetry is reflected after 1900. Modern British and American poets are generously represented; at the same time we have included Africans and Indians, and especially South Africans from the time of Thomas Pringle to that of the Soweto poets. (It is in fact possible to pursue a mini-course on South African poetry using this book.) Though the focus is on verse in English, we have also included, in translation, some examples of African oral poetry, as well as a few French-African, Portuguese-African and Xhosa poems of more recent times.

Accents differs in distinct ways from many other introductory anthologies. It addresses directly the realities of first-year courses, where at the most about forty poems are covered in one year. Similar volumes usually offer extensive selections and large, even cumbersome, formats. We have limited the number of poems to just over 200 (of which approximately half are pre-1900). The selection is sufficiently broad to allow for reasonable variation over several years; at the same time we have managed to produce a compact, relatively inexpensive volume, in which emphasis is accorded our own time and place. While we hope that senior high-school pupils will find value in this book the appeal is primarily to students rather than, simultaneously, to schools and universities. As a result we were able to offer a more lively and diverse selection than might otherwise have been the case. Social as well as individual consciousness is seen as a vital concern; neither have we ignored 'alternative' insights, experiences and responses.

Each of the poems has been tested in the tutorial situation, and most can fruitfully be explored within a single lesson. We have, however, allowed scope for other projects. Wordsworth's 'Tintern Abbey', for example, should encourage exercises in extended analysis. The four poems of Yeats have interesting thematic unities and could initiate a rudimentary examination of a single poet's development. The possibility of a small course on South African poetry has already been mentioned, and other poems may be related to traditional 'periods' (Elizabethan, Romantic, Victorian, etc.). Selections also allow for different emphases of approach: thematic, historical or stylistic. Finally, *Accents* seeks to convey the power of the poetic voice, and we have therefore placed notes at the end and kept extraneous information to a minimum. (Bracketed numbers at the end of certain poems refer to the page numbers on which relevant notes are to be found.)

Several of our colleagues in the Department of English assisted in the selections and in the compilation of notes, and we wish to thank those concerned.

Michael Chapman
Tony Voss
University of Natal
Durban

TRADITIONAL (AFRICAN)

Prayer to the Hunting Star, Canopus
  said by X-nanni

Xkoagu, give me your heart
that you sit with in plenty.
Take my heart, my heart
small and famished without hope
so that like you too I may be full
  for I hunger.

You seem to me full-bellied, Xkoagu
and in my eyes not small
  but I am hungry.

10 Star, give to me your belly
that fills you with a good feeling,
and you shall take my stomach from me
so you as well can know its hunger.
Give me your right arm too
and you shall take my arm from me,
my arm that does not kill
  for I miss my aim.

Xkoagu, blind with your light
  the Springbok's eyes,
20 and you shall give me your arm
for my arm that hangs here
that makes me miss my mark.

(San)

How Death Came

The Moon, they say, called Mantis,
sent him with life to people saying:
Go to men and tell them this —
  As I die and dying live,
  you too shall die and dying live.
Mantis started, took the word.
Then Hare stopped him by the path,

he said: What, insect, is your errand?
Mantis answered: I am sent by Moon,
10 by that one, I must say to men —
> As he dies and dying lives
> they too shall die and dying live.

Hare the quick-tongue said to him:
Why run? You are shaky on your legs.
Let me go, I outrun the wind.
Hare ran, he came to men and said:
Moon sent me with this word —
> As I die and dying perish
> you shall die and utterly die.

20 Hare raced again to Moon,
told him all that he had said to men.
The Moon said dark with anger:
How is it you dared tell them
this thing I never said?
He took up wood, a sharp fire-log,
with one blow in the face
struck down the Hare. He split
the lying Hare's lip to this day.

(Khoikhoi)

Praises of Masellane (a fragment)

Masellane is a self-spreading rock,
spreading itself out from the start.
> A pestle that rattles and jars,
he spoils other people's rhythm,
he stamps though he was not invited.

(Tswana)

(p. 241)

18

Praises of Shaka (a fragment)

Dlungwana son of Ndaba!
    Ferocious one of the Mbelebele brigade,
Who raged among the large kraals,
So that until dawn the huts were being turned upside-down.
    He who is famous as he sits, son of Menzi,
He who beats but is not beaten, unlike water,
Axe that surpasses other axes in sharpness;
Shaka, I fear to say he is Shaka,
Shaka, he is the chief of the Mashobas.
10   He of the shrill whistle, the lion;
He who armed in the forest, who is like a madman,
The madman who is in full view of the men.
He who trudged wearily the plain going to Mfene;
The voracious one of Senzangakhona,
Spear that is red even on the handle.
    The open-handed one, they have matched the regiments,
They were matched by Noju and Ngqengenye,
The one belonging to Ntombazi and the other to Nandi;
He brought out the one with the red brush,
20   Brought out by the white one of Nandi.

(Zulu)

(p. 241)

The Creation Story

At the beginning there was a huge drop of milk.
Then Doondari came and he created the stone.
Then the stone created iron;
And iron created fire;
And fire created water;
And water created air.
Then Doondari descended the second time.
And he took the five elements
And he shaped them into man.
10   But man was proud.
Then Doondari created blindness, and blindness defeated man.

19

But when blindness became too proud,
Doondari created sleep, and sleep defeated blindness;
But when sleep became too proud,
Doondari created worry, and worry defeated sleep;
But when worry became too proud,
Doondari created death, and death defeated worry.
But then death became too proud,
Doondari descended for the third time,
20   And he came as Gueno, the eternal one.
And Gueno defeated death.

(Fulani)

from: *The Holy Bible*
   (Authorised King James Version, 1611)

Psalm 23

1   The Lord is my shepherd; I shall not want.
2   He maketh me to lie down in green pastures: he leadeth me
beside the still waters.
3   He restoreth my soul: he leadeth me in the paths of
righteousness for his name's sake.
4   Yea, though I walk through the valley of the shadow
of death, I will fear no evil: for thou art with me; thy rod and
thy staff they comfort me.
5   Thou preparest a table before me in the presence of mine
enemies: thou anointest my head with oil; my cup runneth over.
6   Surely goodness and mercy shall follow me all the days of
my life: and I will dwell in the house of the Lord for ever.

(A Psalm of David)

Psalm 121

1   I will lift up mine eyes unto the hills, from whence cometh
my help.
2   My help cometh from the Lord, which made heaven and
earth.
3   He will not suffer thy foot to be moved: he that keepeth
thee will not slumber.
4   Behold, he that keepeth Israel shall neither slumber nor
sleep.
5   The Lord is thy keeper: the Lord is thy shade upon thy
right hand.
6   The sun shall not smite thee by day, nor the moon by
night.
7   The Lord shall preserve thee from all evil: he shall preserve
thy soul.
8   The Lord shall preserve thy going out and thy coming
in from this time forth, and even for evermore.

(A Song of Degrees)

from: **The Song of Solomon**

9 What is thy beloved more than another beloved, O thou fairest among women? What is thy beloved more than another beloved, that thou dost so charge us?

10 My beloved is white and ruddy, the chiefest among ten thousand.

11 His head is as the most fine gold, his locks are bushy, and black as a raven.

12 His eyes are as the eyes of doves by the rivers of waters, washed with milk, and fitly set.

13 His cheeks are as a bed of spices, as sweet flowers: his lips like lilies, dropping sweet smelling myrrh.

14 His hands are as gold rings set with the beryl: his belly is as bright ivory overlaid with sapphires.

15 His legs are as pillars of marble, set upon sockets of fine gold: his countenance is as Lebanon, excellent as the cedars.

16 His mouth is most sweet: yea, he is altogether lovely. This is my beloved, and this is my friend, O daughters of Jerusalem.

(5: 9-16)

OLD ENGLISH RIDDLES

a)   I heard of a wonder, of words moth-eaten;
that is a strange thing, I thought, weird
that a man's song be swallowed by a worm,
his binded sentences, his bedside stand-by
rustled in the night — and the robber-guest
not one whit the wiser for the words he had mumbled.

b)   On earth there's a warrior of curious origin.
He's created, gleaming, by two dumb creatures
for the benefit of men. Foe bears him against foe
to inflict harm. Women often fetter him,
strong as he is. If maidens and men
care for him with due consideration
and feed him frequently, he'll faithfully obey them
and serve them well. Men succour him for the warmth
he offers in return; but this warrior will savage
anyone who permits him to become too proud.

c)   The wave, over the wave, a weird thing I saw,
through-wrought, and wonderfully ornate:
a wonder on the wave — water became bone.

(translated into modern English)

(Solutions are given in the Notes, p. 241)

The Wife of Usher's Well

There lived a wife at Usher's Well,
    And a wealthy wife was she;
She had three stout and stalwart sons,
    And sent them oer the sea.

They hadna been a week from her,
    A week but barely ane,
Whan word came to the carline wife
    That her three sons were gane.

They hadna been a week from her,
10   A week but barely three,
Whan word came to the carline wife
    That her sons she'd never see.

'I wish the wind may never cease,
    Nor fashes in the flood,
Till my three sons come hame to me,
    In earthly flesh and blood.'

It fell about the Martinmass,
    When nights are lang and mirk,
The carline wife's three sons came hame,
20   And their hats were o the birk.

It neither grew in syke nor ditch,
    Nor yet in ony sheugh;
But at the gates o Paradise,
    That birk grew fair eneugh.

'Blow up the fire, my maidens,
    Bring water from the well;
For a' my house shall feast this night,
    Since my three sons are well.'

And she has made to them a bed,
30   She's made it large and wide,
And she's taen her mantle her about,
    Sat down at the bed-side.

Up then crew the red, red cock,
    And up and crew the gray;
The eldest to the youngest said,
    ''Tis time we were away.'

The cock he hadna crawd but once,
    And clappd his wings at a',
When the youngest to the eldest said,
40   'Brother, we must awa.

'The cock doth craw, the day doth daw,
    The channerin worm doth chide;
Gin we be mist out o our place,
    A sair pain we maun bide.

'Fare ye weel, my mother dear!
    Fareweel to barn and byre!
And fare ye weel, the bonny lass
    That kindles my mother's fire!'

7 carline, *peasant*; 14 fashes, *storms*; 20 birk, *birch*; 21 syke, *brook*; 22 sheugh, *ditch*; 42 channerin, *gnawing*

Edward

Why dois your brand sae drap wi bluid,
                    Edward, Edward?
Why dois your brand sae drap wi bluid,
     And why sae sad gang yee O?
O I hae killed my hauke sae guid,
                    Mither, mither,
O I hae killed my hauke sae guid,
     And I had nae mair bot hee O.

Your haukis bluid was nevir sae reid,
                    Edward, Edward,
Your haukis bluid was nevir sae reid,
     My deir son I tell thee O.
O I hae killed my reid-roan steid,
10   Mither, mither,
O I hae killed my reid-roan steid,
     That erst was sae fair an frie O.

Your steid was auld, and ye hae gat mair,
                    Edward, Edward,
Your steid was auld, and ye hae gat mair,
     Sum other dule ye drie O.
O I hae killed my fadir deir,
                    Mither, mither,
O I hae killed my fadir deir,
     Alas, and wae is mee O!

And whatten penance wul ye drie for that,
                    Edward, Edward?
20   And whatten penance will ye drie for that?
     My deir son, now tell me O.
Ile set my feit in yonder boat,
                    Mither, mither,
Ile set my feit in yonder boat,
     And Ile fare ovir the sea O.

And what wul ye doe wi your towirs and your ha,
                    Edward, Edward?
And what wul ye doe wi your towirs and your ha,
     That were sae fair to see O?

Ile let thame stand tul they doun fa,
   Mither, mither,
Ile let thame stand tul they doun fa,
30 For here nevir mair maun I bee O.

And what wul ye leive to your bairns and your wife,
   Edward, Edward?
And what wul ye leive to your bairns and your wife,
  Whan ye gang ovir the sea O?
The warldis room, late them beg thrae life,
   Mither, mither,
The warldis room, late them beg thrae life,
  For thame nevir mair wul I see O.

And what wul ye leive to your ain mither deir,
   Edward, Edward?
And what wul ye leive to your ain mither deir?
  My deir son, now tell me O.
40 The curse of hell frae me sall ye beir,
   Mither, mither,
The curse of hell frae me sall ye beir,
  Sic counseils ye gave to me O.

15 dule, *sorrow, grief*; 15, 19 drie, *suffer, undergo*

The Demon Lover

'O where have you been, my long, long love,
    This long seven years and mair?'
'O I'm come to seek my former vows
    Ye granted me before.'

'O hold your tongue of your former vows,
    For they will breed sad strife;
O hold your tongue of your former vows,
    For I am become a wife.'

He turned him right and round about,
10   And the tear blinded his ee:
'I wad never hae trodden on Irish ground,
    If it had not been for thee.

'I might hae had a king's daughter,
    Far, far beyond the sea;
I might have had a king's daughter,
    Had it not been for love o thee.'

'If ye might have had a king's daughter,
    Yer sel ye had to blame;
Ye might have taken the king's daughter,
20   For ye kend that I was nane.

'If I was to leave my husband dear,
    And my two babes also,
O what have you to take me to,
    If with you I should go?'

'I hae seven ships upon the sea —
    The eighth brought me to land —
With four-and-twenty bold mariners,
    And music on every hand.'

She has taken up her two little babes,
30   Kiss'd them baith cheek and chin:
'O fair ye weel, my ain two babes,
    For I'll never see you again.'

She set her foot upon the ship,
    No mariners could she behold;
But the sails were o the taffetie,
    And the masts o the beaten gold.

They had not sailed a league, a league,
    A league but barely three,
When dismal grew his countenance,
40   And drumlie grew his ee.

They had not sailed a league, a league,
    A league but barely three,
Until she espied his cloven foot,
    And she wept right bitterlie.

'O hold your tongue of your weeping,' says he,
    'Of your weeping now let me be;
I will shew you how lilies grow
    On the banks of Italy.'

'O what hills are yon, yon pleasant hills,
50   That the sun shines sweetly on?'
'O yon are the hills of heaven,' he said,
    'Where you will never win.'

'O whaten mountain is yon,' she said,
    'All so dreary wi frost and snow?'
'O yon is the mountain of hell,' he cried
    'Where you and I will go.'

He strack the tap-mast wi his hand,
    The fore-mast wi his knee,
And he brake that gallant ship in twain,
60   And sank her in the sea.

40 drumlie, *gloomy, troubled*

(p. 241)

MEDIEVAL LYRICS

The Singing Maid

Now springes the spray,
All for love I am so seek
That slepen I ne may.

Als I me rode this endre day
O' my pleyinge,
Seih I whar a litel may
Began to singe,
'The clot him clinge!
Way es him i' love-longinge
10   Shall libben ay!'

Son I herde that mirye note,
Thider I drogh:
I fonde hire in an herber swot
Under a bogh,
With joye inogh.
Son I asked, 'Thou mirye may,
Why singes tou ay?'

Than answerde that maiden swote
Midde wordes fewe,
20   'My lemman me haves bihot
Of love trewe:
He chaunges anewe.
Yiif I may, it shall him rewe
By this day!'

(c. 1300)

---

1 *Now (that) the twigs come into leaf;* 4 *As I rode (out) the other day;* 5 Seih, *saw;* 8 *May the earth (of the grave?) cling to him;* 9-10 *Wretched is the man who must live forever in love-longing;* 15 inogh, *a-plenty;* tou, *thou;* 19 Midde, *with;* 20-1 *My beloved had promised his true love to me;* 23-4 *If I can (manage it), he will regret it, by this day*

(p. 241)

I have a gentle cock

I have a gentle cock,
Croweth me day:
He doth me risen erly
My matins for to say.

I have a gentle cock,
Comen he is of gret:
His comb is of red coral,
His tail is of jet.

I have a gentle cock,
10   Comen he is of kinde:
His comb is of red coral,
His tail is of inde.

His legges ben of asor,
So gentle and so smale;
His spores arn of silver whit
Into the wortewale.

His eynen arn of cristal,
Loken all in aumber:
And every night he percheth him
20   In mine ladye's chaumber.

(c. 1400)

---

1 gentle, *noble, well-bred;* 6 gret, *great (lineage);* 10 kinde, *good birth;* 12 inde, *indigo;* 13 asor, *azure;* 14 smale, *delicate* or *slender;* 16 wortewale, *the root (of the spur);* 18 loken, *set*

(p. 241)

Adam lay ibounden

Adam lay ibounden,
Bounden in a bond:
Foure thousand winter
Thought he not too long.
And all was for an apple,
An apple that he tok,
As clerkes finden
Wreten in here book.

Ne hadde the apple take ben,
10   The apple taken ben,
Ne hadde never our Lady
A ben Hevene Quen.
Blissed be the time
That apple take was!
Therfore we moun singen,
'Deo gracias!'

(c. 1400)

1 ibounden, *in bondage*; 7 clerkes, *the learned*; 8 here, *their*; 9 Ne hadde . . .
take ben, *(if)* . . . *had not been taken*; 15 moun, *may*; 16 Deo Gracias, *Thanks be
to God*

(p. 241)

Westron Winde

Westron winde, when will thou blow,
The smalle raine downe can raine?
Christ if my love were in my armes,
And I in my bed againe.

(c. 1500)

GEOFFREY CHAUCER (1340? – 1400)

The Canterbury Tales (extracts)

(A Monk)

A Monk ther was, a fair for the maistrie,
An outridere, that lovede venerie,
A manly man, to been an abbot able.
Ful many a deyntee hors hadde he in stable,
And whan he rood, men myghte his brydel heere
Gynglen in a whistlynge wynd als cleere
And eek as loude as dooth the chapel belle.
Ther as this lord was kepere of the celle,
The reule of seint Maure or of seint Beneit,
By cause that it was old and somdel streit   10
This ilke Monk leet olde thynges pace,
And heeld after the newe world the space.
He yaf nat of that text a pulled hen,
That seith that hunters ben nat hooly men,
Ne that a monk, whan he is reccheees,
Is likned til a fissh that is waterlees, –
This is to seyn, a monk out of his cloystre.
But thilke text heeld he nat worth an oystre;
And I seyde his opinion was good.
What sholde he studie and make hymselven wood,   20
Upon a book in cloystre alwey to poure,
Or swynken with his handes, and laboure,
As Austyn bit? How shal the world be served?
Lat Austyn have his swynk to hym reserved!
Therfore he was a prikasour aright:
Grehoundes he hadde as swift as fowel in flight;
Of prikyng and of huntyng for the hare
Was al his lust, for no cost wolde he spare.
I seigh his sleves purfiled at the hond
With grys, and that the fyneste of a lond;   30
And, for the festne his hood under his chyn,
He hadde of gold ywroght a ful curious pyn;
A love-knotte in the gretter ende ther was.
His heed was balled, that shoon as any glas,
And eek his face, as he hadde been enoynt.

He was a lord ful fat and in good poynt;
His eyen stepe, and rollynge in his heed,
That stemed as a forneys of a leed;
His bootes souple, his hors in greet estaat.
40 Now certeinly he was a fair prelaat;
He was nat pale as a forpyned goost.
A fat swan loved he best of any roost.
His palfrey was as broun as is a berye.

(from: The General Prologue)

1 for the maistrie, *surpassing all others;* 2 outridere, i.e. *he looked after the estates of the monastery;* 2 venerie, *hunting;* 6 gynglen, *jingling;* 8 celle, *a subordinate monastery;* 9 Beneit, *St Benedict, the father of western monasticism (St Maurus, his disciple);* 10 streit, *strict;* 15 recchelees, *regardless of duty/discipline;* 20 wood *mad;* 22 swynken, *work;* 23 As Austyn bit, *as St Augustine instructed* 25 prikasour, *hunter on horseback;* 27 prikyng, *following a hare by its tracks* 29 seigh ... purfild, *saw ... trimmed at the edges;* 30 grys, *costly grey fur;* 37 stepe, *large, protruding;* 38 leed, *cauldron;* 41 forpyned, *tormented;* 43 palfrey, *riding horse*

(Chauntecleer)

       . . . a cok, hight Chauntecleer.
In al the land, of crowyng nas his peer.
His voys was murier than the murie orgon
On messe-dayes that in the chirche gon.
Wel sikerer was his crowyng in his logge
Than is a clokke or an abbey orlogge.
By nature he knew ech ascencioun
Of the equynoxial in thilke toun;
For whan degrees fiftene weren ascended,
10 Thanne crew he, that it myghte nat been amended.
His coomb was redder than the fyn coral.
And batailled as it were a castel wal;
His byle was blak, and as the jeet it shoon;
Lyk asure were his legges and his toon;
His nayles whitter than the lylye flour,
And lyk the burned gold was his colour.
This gentil cok hadde in his governaunce
Sevene hennes for to doon al his plesaunce,
Whiche were his sustres and his paramours,
20 And wonder lyk to hym, as of colours;
Of whiche the faireste hewed on hir throte
Was cleped faire damoysele Pertelote.
Curteys she was, discreet, and debonaire,
And compaignable, and bar hyrself so faire,
Syn thilke day that she was seven nyght oold,
That trewely she hath the herte in hoold
Of Chauntecleer, loken in every lith;
He loved hire so that wel was hym therwith.
But swich a joye was it to here hem synge,
30 Whan that the brighte sonne gan to sprynge,
In sweete accord, 'My lief is faren in londe!'
For thilke tyme, as I have understonde,
Beestes and briddes koude speke and synge.

(*from*: The Nun's Priest's Tale)

hight, *called;* 7-8 i.e. *Chauntecleer would crow, by instinct, exactly on the hour;*
27 loken in every lith, *locked in every limb;* 31 My lief is faren in londe, *My
beloved has travelled far (away from me) into the country*
p. 242)

35

Truth

Flee fro the prees, and dwelle with sothfastnesse,
Suffyce unto thy good, though it be smal;
For hord hath hate, and climbing tikelnesse,
Prees hath envye, and wele blent overal;
Savour no more than thee bihove shal;
Reule wel thyself, that other folk canst rede;
And trouthe thee shal delivere, it is no drede.

Tempest thee noght al croked to redresse,
In trust of hir that turneth as a bal:
10   Gret reste stant in litel besinesse;
Be war also to sporne ayeyns an al;
Stryve not, as doth the crokke with the wal.
Daunte thyself, that dauntest otheres dede;
And trouthe thee shal delivere, it is no drede.

That thee is sent, receyve in buxumnesse;
The wrastling for this world axeth a fal.
Her is non hoom, her nis but wildernesse:
Forth, pilgrim, forth! Forth, beste, out of thy stal!
Know thy contree, look up, thank God of al;
20   Hold the heye wey, and lat thy gost thee lede;
And trouthe thee shal delivere, it is no drede.

Envoy

Therfore, thou Vache, leve thyn old wrecchednesse;
Unto the world leve now to be thral;
Crye him mercy, that of his hy goodnesse
Made thee of noght, and in especial
Draw unto him, and pray in general
For thee, and eek for other, hevenlich mede.
And trouthe thee shal delivere, it is no drede.

1 prees, *throng;* tikelnesse, *insecurity;* 4 blent, *blinds;* 6 rede, *advise;* 9 hir that turneth, i.e. *Fortune;* 11 al, *awl;* 12 crokke, *earthenware pot;* 13 daunte, *govern;* 22 Vache, *(Fr.) cow (the poem may have been addressed to Sir Philip de la Vache);* 23 leve, *cease;* 28 mede, *reward*

The Complaint of Chaucer to his Purse

To yow, my purse, and to noon other wight
Complayne I, for ye be my lady dere!
I am so sory, now that ye been lyght;
For certes, but ye make me hevy chere,
Me were as leef be layd upon my bere;
For which unto your mercy thus I crye:
Beth hevy ageyn, or elles moot I dye!

Now voucheth sauf this day, or yt be nyght,
That I of yow the blisful soun may here,
10   Or see your colour lyk the sonne bryght,
That of yelownesse hadde never pere.
Ye be my lyf, ye be myn hertes stere,
Quene of comfort and of good companye:
Beth hevy ageyn, or elles moot I dye!

Now purse, that ben to me my lyves lyght
And saveour, as doun in this world here,
Out of this toune helpe me thurgh your myght,
Syn that ye wole nat ben my tresorere;
For I am shave as nye as any frere.
20   But yet I pray unto your curtesye:
Beth hevy agen, or elles moot I dye!

Lenvoy de Chaucer

O conquerour of Brutes Albyon,
Which that by lyne and free eleccion
Been verray kyng, this song to yow I sende;
And ye, that mowen alle oure harmes amende,
Have mynde upon my supplicacion!

1 wight, *person;* 3 lyght, *light, fickle;* 8 or, *before;* 12 stere, *rudder;* 24 lyne, *lineage*
(p. 242)

JOHN SKELTON (1460?—1529)

To Mistress Margaret Hussey

> Merry Margaret,
>   As midsummer flower,
> Gentle as falcon
> Or hawk of the tower:
> With solace and gladness,
> Much mirth and no madness,
> All good and no badness;
>   So joyously,
>   So maidenly,
10 So womanly
>   Her demeaning
>   In every thing,
>   Far, far passing
>   That I can indite,
>   Or suffice to write
> Of Merry Margaret
>   As midsummer flower,
> Gentle as falcon
> Or hawk of the tower.
20   As patient and still
> And as full of good will
> As fair Isaphill,
>   Coriander,
>   Sweet pomander,
>   Good Cassander,
>   Steadfast of thought,
>   Well made, well wrought,
>   Far may be sought
>   Ere that ye can find
30 So courteous, so kind
> As Merry Margaret,
>   This midsummer flower,
> Gentle as falcon
> Or hawk of the tower.

3 gentle as falcon, *well-born (falcons were noble hunting-birds)*; 4 hawk of the
tower, i.e. *before swooping on its prey, the hawk towers (flies high in the air)*

(p. 242)

SIR THOMAS WYATT (1503 – 1542)

They Flee from Me

They flee from me, that sometime did me seek,
With naked foot stalking in my chamber.
I have seen them, gentle, tame, and meek,
That now are wild, and do not remember
That sometime they put themselves in danger
To take bread at my hand, and now they range,
Busily seeking with a continual change.

Thanked be Fortune it hath been otherwise,
Twenty times better; but once in special,
10   In thin array, after a pleasant guise,
When her loose gown from her shoulders did fall,
And she me caught in her arms long and small,
And therewith all sweetly did me kiss
And softly said, 'Dear heart, how like you this?'

It was no dream, I lay broad waking.
But all is turned, thorough my gentleness,
Into a strange fashion of forsaking;
And I have leave to go, of her goodness,
And she also to use newfangleness.
20   But since that I so kindely am served,
I fain would know what she hath deserved.

(p. 242)

Whoso List to Hunt

Whoso list to hunt, I know where is an hind,
   But as for me alas, I may no more –
   The vain travail hath wearied me so sore,
   I am of them that farthest cometh behind.
Yet may I, by no means, my wearied mind
   Draw from the deer, but as she fleeth afore,
   Fainting I follow. I leave off therefore,
   Since in a net I seek to hold the wind.

Who list her hunt, I put him out of doubt,
10   As well as I, may spend his time in vain.
        And graven with diamonds in letters plain
There is written her fair neck round about:
        'Noli me tangere, for Caesar's I am,
        And wild for to hold, though I seem tame.'

13 Don't touch me
(p. 242)

I Find No Peace

I find no peace and all my war is done;
        I fear and hope, I burn and freeze like ice;
        I fly above the wind, yet can I not arise,
        And naught I have and all the world I seize on;
That looseth nor locketh holdeth me in prison,
        And holdeth me not yet can I scape nowise;
        Nor letteth me live nor die at my devise,
        And yet of death it giveth none occasion.
Without eyen I see, and without tongue I plain;
10   I desire to perish, and yet I ask health;
        I love another, and thus I hate myself;
        I feed me in sorrow, and laugh in all my pain.
        Likewise displeaseth me both death and life,
        And my delight is causer of this strife.

(p. 242)

CHIDIOCK TICHBORNE (1558? – 1586)

Tichborne's Elegy

My prime of youth is but a frost of cares,
My feast of joy is but a dish of pain,
My crop of corn is but a field of tares,
And all my good is but vain hope of gain;
The day is past, and yet I saw no sun,
And now I live, and now my life is done.

My tale was heard and yet it was not told,
My fruit is fallen and yet my leaves are green,
My youth is spent and yet I am not old,
10   I saw the world and yet I was not seen;
My thread is cut and yet it is not spun,
And now I live, and now my life is done.

I sought my death and found it in my womb,
I looked for life and saw it was a shade,
I trod the earth and knew it was my tomb,
And now I die, and now I was but made;
My glass is full, and now my glass is run,
And now I live, and now my life is done.

(p. 242)

SONGS

The silver Swan, who living had no Note

The silver Swan, who living had no Note,
When death approacht unlockt her silent throat,
Leaning her breast against the reedy shore,
Thus sung her first and last, and sung no more:
Farewell all joys, O death come close mine eyes,
More Geese than Swans now live, more fools than wise.

(p. 242)

Weep you no more sad fountains

1

Weep you no more sad fountains,
    What need you flow so fast,
Look how the snowy mountains,
    Heav'n's sun doth gently waste.
But my sun's heav'nly eyes
    View not your weeping,
    That now lies sleeping
Softly, now softly lies
    Sleeping.

2

10   Sleep is a reconciling,
    A rest that peace begets:
Doth not the sun rise smiling,
    When fair at ev'n he sets,
Rest you, then rest sad eyes,
    Melt not in weeping,
    While she lies sleeping
Softy, now softly lies
    Sleeping.

(p. 242)

SIR WALTER RALEGH (1552?—1618)

As you came from the holy land
(Sometimes attributed to Ralegh)

'As you came from the holy land
   Of Walsinghame,
Met you not with my true love
   By the way as you came?'

'How shall I know your true love,
   That have met many one
As I went to the holy land,
   That have come, that have gone?'

'She is neither white nor brown,
10   But as the heavens fair:
There is none hath a form so divine
   In the earth or the air.'

'Such an one did I meet, good Sir,
   Such an angelic face,
Who like a queen, like a nymph, did appear,
   By her gait, by her grace.'

'She hath left me here all alone,
   All alone as unknown,
Who sometimes did me lead with her self
20   And me loved as her own.'

'What's the cause that she leaves you alone
   And a new way doth take:
Who loved you once as her own,
   And her joy did you make?'

'I have loved her all my youth,
   But, now old as you see,
Love likes not the falling fruit
   From the withered tree.'

'Know that love is a careless child
30   And forgets promise past:
He is blind, he is deaf, when he list
     And in faith never fast.

'His desire is a dureless content
     And a trustless joy;
He is won with a world of despair
     And is lost with a toy.'

'Of women kind such indeed is the love
     Or the word Love abused,
Under which many childish desires
40   And conceits are excused.

'But Love is a durable fire,
     In the mind ever burning:
Never sick, never old, never dead,
     From itself never turning.'

(p. 243)

On the Life of Man

What is our life? a play of passion,
Our mirth the music of division;
Our mothers' wombs the tiring-houses be
Where we are dressed for this short comedy;
Heaven the judicious, sharp spectator is
That sits and marks still who doth act amiss;
Our graves that hide us from the searching sun
Are like drawn curtains when the play is done:
Thus march we, playing, to our latest rest,
Only we die in earnest, that's no jest.

(p. 243)

EDMUND SPENSER (1552?–1599)

More than most fair, full of the living fire

More than most fair, full of the living fire,
Kindled above unto the Maker near;
No eyes but joys, in which all powers conspire,
That to the world nought else be counted dear;
Through your bright beams doth not the blinded guest
Shoot out his darts to base affections wound;
But angels come to lead frail minds to rest
In chaste desires, on heavenly beauty bound.
You frame my thoughts, and fashion me within;
10   You stop my tongue, and teach my heart to speak;
You calm the storm that passion did begin,
Strong through your cause, but by your virtue weak.
    Dark is the world, where your light shinèd never;
    Well is he born, that may behold you ever.

(*Amoretti*: 8)

(p. 243)

One day I wrote her name upon the strand

One day I wrote her name upon the strand,
    but came the waves and washèd it away:
    again I wrote it with a second hand,
    but came the tide, and made my pains his prey.
Vain man, said she, that dost in vain assay,
    a mortal thing so to immortalize,
    for I myself shall like to this decay,
    and eek my name be wipèd out likewise.
Not so, (quod I) let baser things devise
10   to die in dust, but you shall live by fame:
    my verse your virtues rare shall eternize,
    and in the heavens write your glorious name.
Where whenas death shall all the world subdue,
    our love shall live, and later life renew.

(p. 243)

SIR PHILIP SIDNEY (1554–1586)

With how sad steps, O Moon, thou climb'st the skies!

With how sad steps, O Moon, thou climb'st the skies!
How silently, and with how wan a face!
What, may it be that even in heavenly place
That busy archer his sharp arrows tries!
Sure, if that long-with-love-acquainted eyes
Can judge of love, thou feel'st a lover's case,
I read it in thy looks; thy languished grace,
To me, that feel the like, thy state descries.
Then, even of fellowship, O Moon, tell me,
10   Is constant love deemed there but want of wit?
Are beauties there as proud as here they be?
Do they above love to be loved, and yet
Those lovers scorn whom that love doth possess?
Do they call virtue there ungratefulness?

   (from: *Astrophel and Stella*)

(p. 243)

Oft have I mused, but now at length I find

Oft have I mused, but now at length I find,
   Why those that die, men say they do depart.
'Depart!' — a word so gentle, to my mind,
   Weakly did seem to paint death's ugly dart.
But now the stars, with their strange course, do bind
   Me one to leave, with whom I leave my heart;
I hear a cry of spirits faint and blind,
   That, parting thus, my chiefest part I part.
Part of my life, the loathèd part to me,
10   Lives to impart my weary clay some breath;
But that good part, wherein all comforts be,
     Now dead, doth show departure is a death —
       Yea, worse than death; death parts both woe and joy.
       From joy I part, still living in annoy.

(p. 243)

46

WILLIAM SHAKESPEARE (1564–1616)

That time of year thou mayst in me behold

That time of year thou mayst in me behold
When yellow leaves, or none, or few, do hang
Upon those boughs which shake against the cold,
Bare ruined choirs where late the sweet birds sang:
In me thou see'st the twilight of such day
As after sunset fadeth in the west,
Which by and by black night doth take away,
Death's second self that seals up all in rest:
In me thou see'st the glowing of such fire
10   That on the ashes of his youth doth lie
As the death-bed whereon it must expire,
Consumed with that which it was nourished by:
    This thou perceivest, which makes thy love more strong
    To love that well which thou must leave ere long.

They that have power to hurt and will do none

They that have power to hurt and will do none,
That do not do the thing they most do show,
Who moving others are themselves as stone,
Unmovèd, cold, and to temptation slow;
They rightly do inherit heaven's graces,
And husband nature's riches from expense;
They are the lords and owners of their faces,
Others but stewards of their excellence.
The summer's flower is to the summer sweet,
10   Though to itself it only live and die;
But if that flower with base infection meet,
The basest weed outbraves his dignity:
    For sweetest things turn sourest by their deeds.
    Lilies that fester smell far worse than weeds.

(p. 243)

When my love swears that she is made of truth

When my love swears that she is made of truth
I do believe her, though I know she lies,
That she might think me some untutored youth
Unlearnèd in the world's false subtleties.
Thus vainly thinking that she thinks me young,
Although she knows my days are past the best,
Simply I credit her false-speaking tongue:
On both sides thus is simple truth suppressed.
But wherefore says she not she is unjust?
10 And wherefore say not I that I am old?
Oh, love's best habit is in seeming trust,
And age, in love, loves not to have years told.
    Therefore I lie with her, and she with me,
    And in our faults by lies we flattered be.

(p. 243)

Let me not to the marriage of true minds

Let me not to the marriage of true minds
Admit impediments: love is not love
Which alters when it alteration finds,
Or bends with the remover to remove.
Oh no! it is an ever-fixèd mark
That looks on tempests and is never shaken;
It is the star to every wandering bark,
Whose worth's unknown although his height be taken.
Love's not Time's fool, though rosy lips and cheeks
10 Within his bending sickle's compass come;
Love alters not with his brief hours and weeks,
But bears it out even to the edge of doom.
    If this be error and upon me proved,
    I never writ, nor no man ever loved.

Not marble, nor the gilded monuments

Not marble, nor the gilded monuments
Of princes shall outlive this powerful rhyme;
But you shall shine more bright in these contents
Than unswept stone besmeared with sluttish time.
When wasteful war shall statues overturn,
And broils root out the work of masonry,
Nor Mars his sword nor war's quick fire shall burn
The living record of your memory.
'Gainst death and all oblivious enmity
10   Shall you pace forth: your praise shall still find room
Even in the eyes of all posterity
That wear this world out to the ending doom.
      So, till the judgement that yourself arise,
      You live in this, and dwell in lovers' eyes.

(p. 243)

Fear no more the heat o' th' sun

Fear no more the heat o' th' sun
      Nor the furious winter's rages;
Thou thy worldly task hast done,
      Home art gone, and ta'en thy wages.
Golden lads and girls all must,
As chimney-sweepers, come to dust.

Fear no more the frown o' th' great;
      Thou art past the tyrant's stroke.
Care no more to clothe and eat;
10   To thee the reed is as the oak.
The sceptre, learning, physic, must
All follow this and come to dust.

Fear no more the lightning flash,
    Nor th' all-dreaded thunder-stone;
Fear not slander, censure rash;
    Thou hast finish'd joy and moan.
All lovers young, all lovers must
Consign to thee and come to dust.

20 No exorciser harm thee!
    Nor no witchcraft charm thee!
    Ghost unlaid forbear thee!
    Nothing ill come near thee!
    Quiet consummation have,
    And renowned be thy grave!

(Dirge from *Cymbeline*)

THOMAS NASHE (1567–1601?)

Litany in Time of Plague

Adieu, farewell earth's bliss,
This world uncertain is:
Fond are life's lustful joys,
Death proves them all but toys,
None from his darts can fly.
I am sick, I must die.
  Lord, have mercy on us!

Rich men, trust not in wealth,
Gold cannot buy you health;
10 Physic himself must fade,
All things to end are made.
The plague full swift goes by.
I am sick, I must die.
  Lord, have mercy on us!

Beauty is but a flower
Which wrinkles will devour;
Brightness falls from the air,
Queens have died young and fair,
Dust hath closed Helen's eye.
20 I am sick, I must die.
  Lord, have mercy on us!

Strength stoops unto the grave,
Worms feed on Hector brave,
Swords may not fight with fate,
Earth still holds ope her gate.
Come! come! the bells do cry.
I am sick, I must die.
  Lord, have mercy on us!

Wit with his wantonness
30 Tasteth death's bitterness;
Hell's executioner
Hath no ears for to hear
What vain art can reply.
I am sick, I must die.
  Lord, have mercy on us!

Haste, therefore, each degree,
To welcome destiny.
Heaven is our heritage,
Earth but a player's stage;
40   Mount we unto the sky.
I am sick, I must die.
        Lord, have mercy on us!

(p. 243)

JOHN DONNE (1572–1631)

Sweetest love, I do not go

Sweetest love, I do not go
    For weariness of thee,
Nor in hope the world can show
    A fitter love for me;
        But since that I
Must die at last, 'tis best
To use myself in jest,
    Thus by feigned deaths to die.

Yesternight the sun went hence,
10   And yet is here today;
He hath no desire nor sense,
    Nor half so short a way:
        Then fear not me,
But believe that I shall make
Speedier journeys, since I take
    More wings and spurs than he.

O how feeble is man's power,
    That if good fortune fall,
Cannot add another hour,
20   Nor a lost hour recall!
        But come bad chance,
And we join to it our strength,
And we teach it art and length,
    Itself o'er us to advance.

When thou sigh'st, thou sigh'st not wind,
    But sigh'st my soul away;
When thou weep'st, unkindly kind,
    My life's blood doth decay.
        It cannot be
30 That thou lov'st me, as thou say'st,
If in thine my life thou waste;
    Thou art the best of me.

Let not thy divining heart
    Forethink me any ill;
Destiny may take thy part
    And may thy fears fulfil;
      But think that we
Are but turned aside to sleep;
They who one another keep
40   Alive, ne'er parted be.

(p. 244)

A Valediction: Forbidding Mourning

As virtuous men pass mildly away,
    And whisper to their souls to go,
Whilst some of their sad friends do say
    The breath goes now, and some say, No;

So let us melt, and make no noise,
    No tear-floods, nor sigh-tempests move,
'Twere profanation of our joys
    To tell the laity our love.

Moving of th' earth brings harms and fears,
10   Men reckon what it did and meant;
But trepidation of the spheres,
      Though greater far, is innocent.

Dull sublunary lovers' love
    (Whose soul is sense) cannot admit
Absence, because it doth remove
    Those things which elemented it.

But we by a love so much refined
    That our selves know not what it is,
Inter-assurèd of the mind,
20   Care less, eyes, lips, and hands to miss.

Our two souls therefore, which are one,
    Though I must go, endure not yet
A breach, but an expansion,
    Like gold to airy thinness beat.

If they be two, they are two so
    As stiff twin compasses are two;
Thy soul, the fixed foot, makes no show
    To move, but doth, if th' other do.

And though it in the centre sit,
30   Yet when the other far doth roam,
It leans and hearkens after it,
    And grows erect, as that comes home.

Such wilt thou be to me, who must
    Like th' other foot, obliquely run;
Thy firmness makes my circle just,
    And makes me end where I begun.

(p. 244)

Thou hast made me, and shall thy work decay?

Thou hast made me, and shall thy work decay?
Repair me now, for now mine end doth haste,
I run to death, and death meets me as fast,
And all my pleasures are like yesterday;
I dare not move my dim eyes any way,
Despair behind, and death before doth cast
Such terror, and my feeble flesh doth waste
By sin in it, which it t'wards hell doth weigh;
Only thou art above, and when towards thee
10 By thy leave I can look, I rise again;
But our old subtle foe so tempteth me,
That not one hour myself I can sustain;
Thy Grace may wing me to prevent his art,
And thou like adamant draw mine iron heart.

5

BEN JONSON (1572 – 1637)

Still to be neat, still to be dressed

Still to be neat, still to be dressed,
As you were going to a feast;
Still to be powdered, still perfumed;
Lady, it is to be presumed,
Though art's hid causes are not found,
All is not sweet, all is not sound.

Give me a look, give me a face
That makes simplicity a grace;
Robes loosely flowing, hair as free;
10   Such sweet neglect more taketh me
Then all th' adulteries of art.
They strike mine eyes, but not my heart.

(p. 244)

Epistle. To my Lady Covell

You won not verses, Madam, you won me,
When you would play so nobly, and so free,
A book to a few lines: but, it was fit
You won them too, your odds did merit it.
So have you gain'd a servant, and a Muse:
The first of which I fear, you will refuse;
And you may justly, being a tardy, cold,
Unprofitable chattel, fat and old,
Laden with belly, and doth hardly approach
10   His friends, but to break chairs, or crack a coach.
His weight is twenty stone within two pound;
And that's made up as doth the purse abound.
Marry, the Muse is one, can tread the air,
And stroke the water, nimble, chaste, and fair,
Sleep in a virgin's bosom without fear,
Run all the rounds in a soft lady's ear,
Widow or wife, without the jealousy
Of either suitor, or a servant by.

Such, (if her manners like you) I do send:
20 And can for other graces her commend,
To make you merry on the dressing stool,
A mornings, and at afternoons, to fool
Away ill company, and help in rime
Your Joan to pass her melancholy time.
By this, although you fancy not the man,
Accept his Muse; and tell, I know you can:
How many verses, Madam, are your due!
I can lose none in tend'ring these to you.
I gain, in having leave to keep my day,
30 And should grow rich, had I much more to pay.

(p. 244)

On my First Son

Farewell, thou child of my right hand and joy,
My sin was too much hope of thee, loved boy;
Seven years thou wert lent to me, and I thee pay,
Exacted by thy fate, on the just day.
O, could I lose all father, now. For why
Will man lament the state he should envy?
To have so soon scaped world's and flesh's rage,
And, if no other misery, yet age?
Rest in soft peace, and, asked, say here doth lie
10 Ben Jonson his best piece of poetry.
For whose sake, henceforth, all his vows be such,
As what he loves may never like too much.

(p. 244)

On Spies

Spies, you are lights in state, but of base stuff,
Who, when you have burnt yourselves down to the snuff,
Stink, and are thrown away. End fair enough.

(p. 244)

ROBERT HERRICK (1591–1674)

Delight in Disorder

A sweet disorder in the dress
Kindles in clothes a wantonness.
A lawn about the shoulders thrown
Into a fine distraction;
An erring lace, which here and there
Enthralls the crimson stomacher;
A cuff neglectful, and thereby
Ribbons to flow confusedly;
A winning wave, deserving note,
In the tempestuous petticoat;
A careless shoestring, in whose tie
I see a wild civility;
Do more bewitch me than when art
Is too precise in every part.

(p. 244)

To the Virgins, To Make Much of Time

Gather ye rosebuds while ye may,
    Old time is still a-flying;
And this same flower that smiles today
    Tomorrow will be dying.

The glorious lamp of heaven, the sun,
    The higher he's a-getting,
The sooner will his race be run,
    And nearer he's to setting.

That age is best which is the first,
    When youth and blood are warmer;
But being spent, the worse, and worst
    Times still succeed the former.

Then be not coy, but use your time,
    And, while ye may, go marry;
For, having lost but once your prime,
    You may forever tarry.

GEORGE HERBERT (1593–1633)

Redemption

Having been tenant long to a rich lord,
   Not thriving, I resolvèd to be bold,
     And make a suit unto him, to afford
A new small-rented lease, and cancel th' old.
In heaven at his manor I him sought:
     They told me there, that he was lately gone
     About some land, which he had dearly bought
Long since on earth, to take possession.
I straight returned, and knowing his great birth,
     Sought him accordingly in great resorts;
     In cities, theatres, gardens, parks, and courts;
At length I heard a ragged noise and mirth
     Of thieves and murderers: there I him espied,
     Who straight, *Your suit is granted*, said, and died.

Denial

When my devotions could not pierce
     Thy silent ears;
Then was my heart broken, as was my verse:
     My breast was full of fears
        And disorder:

My bent thoughts, like a brittle bow,
     Did fly asunder:
Each took his way; some would to pleasures go,
     Some to the wars and thunder
        Of alarms.

As good go any where, they say,
     As to benumb
Both knees and heart, in crying night and day,
     Come, come, my God, O come,
        But no hearing.

O that thou shouldst give dust a tongue
    To cry to thee,
And then not hear it crying! all day long
    My heart was in my knee,
20   But no hearing.

Therefore my soul lay out of sight,
    Untun'd, unstrung:
My feeble spirit, unable to look right,
    Like a nipt blossom, hung
            Discontented.

O cheer and tune my heartless breast,
    Defer no time;
That so thy favours granting my request,
    They and my mind may chime,
30   And mend my rime.

(p. 244)

Virtue

Sweet day, so cool, so calm, so bright,
    The bridal of the earth and sky:
The dew shall weep thy fall tonight;
    For thou must die.

Sweet rose, whose hue, angry and brave,
    Bids the rash gazer wipe his eye:
Thy root is ever in its grave,
    And thou must die.

Sweet spring, full of sweet days and roses,
10   A box where sweets compacted lie;
My music shows ye have your closes,
    And all must die.

Only a sweet and virtuous soul,
    Like seasoned timber, never gives;
But though the whole world turn to coal,
    Then chiefly lives.

(p. 244)

Prayer

Prayer, the Church's banquet, Angels' age,
    God's breath in man returning to his birth,
The soul in paraphrase, heart in pilgrimage,
    The Christian plummet, sounding heaven and earth;
Engine against the Almighty, sinner's tower,
    Reversèd thunder, Christ-side-piercing spear,
The six-days' world transposing in an hour,
    A kind of tune, which all things hear and fear;

Softness, and peace, and joy, and love, and bliss,
    Exalted manna, gladness of the best,
    Heaven in ordinary, man well drest,
The milky way, the bird of Paradise,
        Church-bells beyond the stars heard, the soul's blood,
        The land of spices; something understood.

JOHN MILTON (1608–1674)

Paradise Lost (extracts)

(Satan)

Him the Almighty Power
Hurled headlong flaming from th' ethereal sky
With hideous ruin and combustion down
To bottomless perdition, there to dwell
In adamantine chains and penal fire,
Who durst defy th' Omnipotent to arms.
Nine times the space that measures day and night
To mortal men, he with his horrid crew
Lay vanquished, rolling in the fiery gulf
10 Confounded though immortal. But his doom
Reserved him to more wrath; for now the thought
Both of lost happiness and lasting pain
Torments him; round he throws his baleful eyes,
That witnessed huge affliction and dismay
Mixed with obdúrate pride and steadfast hate.
At once as far as angels ken he views
The dismal situation waste and wild
A dungeon horrible, on all sides round
As one great furnace flamed, yet from those flames
20 No light, but rather darkness visible
Served only to discover sights of woe,
Regions of sorrow, doleful shades, where peace
And rest can never dwell, hope never comes
That comes to all; but torture without end
Still urges, and a fiery deluge, fed
With ever-burning sulphur unconsumed:
Such place Eternal Justice had prepared
For those rebellious, here their prison ordained
In utter darkness, and their portion set
30 As far removed from God and light of heav'n
As from the centre thrice to th' utmost pole.
O how unlike the place from whence they fell!
. . .

'Is this the region, this the soil, the clime,'
Said then the lost Archangel, 'this the seat

That we must change for heav'n, this mournful gloom
For that celestial light? Be it so, since he
Who now is sovran can dispose and bid
What shall be right: fardest from him is best,
Whom reason hath equalled, force hath made supreme
40   Above his equals. Farewell, happy fields,
Where joy for ever dwells! Hail, horrors, hail,
Infernal world, and thou, profoundest hell,
Receive they new possessor: one who brings
A mind not to be changed by place or time.
The mind is its own place, and in itself
Can make a heav'n of hell, a hell of heav'n.
What matter where, if I be still the same,
And what I should be, all but less than he
Whom thunder hath made greater? Here at least
50   We shall be free; th' Almighty hath not built
Here for his envy, will not drive us hence:
Here we may reign secure, and in my choice
To reign is worth ambition, though in hell:
Better to reign in hell than serve in heav'n.

(p. 244)

(Adam and Eve)

Two of far nobler shape erect and tall,
God-like erect, with native honour clad
In naked majesty seemed lords of all,
And worthy seemed, for in their looks divine
The image of their glorious Maker shone,
Truth, wisdom, sanctitude severe and pure,
Severe but in true filial freedom placed;
Whence true authority in men; though both
Not equal, as their sex not equal seemed;
10   For contemplation he and valour formed,
For softness she and sweet attractive grace;
He for God only, she for God in him.
His fair large front and eye sublime declared
Absolute rule; and hyacinthine locks
Round from his parted forelock manly hung
Clustering, but not beneath his shoulders broad:

She as a veil down to the slender waist
Her unadornèd golden tresses wore
Disheveled, but in wanton ringlets waved
20   As the vine curls her tendrils, which implied
Subjection, but required with gentle sway,
And by her yielded, by him best received,
Yielded with coy submission, modest pride,
And sweet reluctant amorous delay.
Nor those mysterious parts were then concealed;
Then was not guilty shame, dishonest shame
Of Nature's works, honour dishonorable,
Sin-bred, how have ye troubled all mankind
With shows instead, mere shows of seeming pure,
30   And banished from man's life his happiest life,
Simplicity and spotless innocence.
So passed they naked on, nor shunned the sight
Of God or angel, for they thought no ill;
So hand in hand they passed, the loveliest pair
That ever since in love's embraces met:
Adam the goodliest man of men since born
His sons, the fairest of her daughters Eve.

When I consider how my light is spent

When I consider how my light is spent,
    Ere half my days, in this dark world and wide,
    And that one talent which is death to hide
    Lodged with me useless, though my soul more bent
To serve therewith my maker, and present
    My true account, lest he, returning, chide.
    'Doth God exact day-labour, light denied?'
    I fondly ask; but Patience, to prevent
That murmur, soon replies: 'God doth not need
10   Either man's work or his own gifts, who best
    Bear his mild yoke, they serve him best; his state
Is kingly — thousands at his bidding speed
    And post o'er land and ocean without rest;
They also serve who only stand and wait.'

(p. 245)

SIR JOHN SUCKLING (1609–1642)

Out upon It!

Out upon it! I have loved
   Three whole days together;
And am like to love three more,
   If it prove fair weather.

Time shall moult away his wings,
   Ere he shall discover
In the whole wide world again
   Such a constant lover.

But the spite on't is, no praise
10   Is due at all to me:
Love with me had made no stays
   Had it any been but she.

Had it any been but she,
   And that very face,
There had been at least ere this
   A dozen dozen in her place.

(p. 245)

ANDREW MARVELL (1621 – 1678)

To his Coy Mistress

  Had we but world enough, and time,
This coyness, Lady, were no crime.
We would sit down, and think which way
To walk, and pass our long love's day.
Thou by the Indian Ganges' side
Shouldst rubies find; I by the tide
Of Humber would complain. I would
Love you ten years before the Flood,
And you should, if you please, refuse
10 Till the Conversion of the Jews.
My vegetable love should grow
Vaster than empires and more slow;
An hundred years should go to praise
Thine eyes, and on thy forehead gaze;
Two hundred to adore each breast,
But thirty thousand to the rest;
An age at least to every part,
And the last age should show your heart,
For, Lady, you deserve this state,
20 Nor would I love at lower rate.
  But at my back I always hear
Time's wingèd chariot hurrying near;
And yonder all before us lie
Deserts of vast eternity.
Thy beauty shall no more be found,
Nor, in thy marble vault, shall sound
My echoing song; then worms shall try
That long-preserved virginity,
And your quaint honour turn to dust,
30 And into ashes all my lust:
The grave's a fine and private place,
But none, I think, do there embrace.
  Now therefore, while the youthful hue
Sits on thy skin like morning dew,
And while thy willing soul transpires
At every pore with instant fires,
Now let us sport us while we may,
And now, like amorous birds of prey,

Rather at once our time devour
40 Than languish in his slow-chapt power.
Let us roll all our strength and all
Our sweetness up into one ball,
And tear our pleasures with rough strife
Thorough the iron gates of life;
Thus, though we cannot make our sun
Stand still, yet we will make him run.

(p. 245)

Bermudas

Where the remote Bermudas ride,
In th' ocean's bosom unespied,
From a small boat that rowed along,
The listening winds received this song:
    'What should we do but sing His praise,
That led us through the watery maze
Unto an isle so long unknown,
And yet far kinder than our own?
Where He the huge sea monsters wracks,
10 That lift the deep upon their backs;
He lands us on a grassy stage,
Safe from the storms, and prelate's rage.
He gave us this eternal spring
Which here enamels everything,
And sends the fowls to us in care,
On daily visits through the air;
He hangs in shades the orange bright,
Like golden lamps in a green night,
And does in the pomegranates close
20 Jewels more rich than Ormus shows;
He makes the figs our mouths to meet,
And throws the melons at our feet;
But apples plants of such a price,
No tree could ever bear them twice;
With cedars, chosen by His hand,
From Lebanon, He stores the land;
And makes the hollow seas, that roar,
Proclaim the ambergris on shore;

He cast (of which we rather boast)
30   The Gospel's pearl upon our coast,
And in these rocks for us did frame
A temple, where to sound His name.
O! let our voice His praise exalt,
Till it arrive at heaven's vault,
Which, thence (perhaps) rebounding, may
Echo beyond the Mexique Bay.'
        Thus sung they in the English boat,
An holy and a cheerful note;
And all the way, to guide their chime,
40   With falling oars they kept the time.

(p. 245)

HENRY VAUGHAN (1622 – 1695)

The Retreat

Happy those early days! when I
Shined in my angel infancy.
Before I understood this place
Appointed for my second race,
Or taught my soul to fancy aught
But a white, celestial thought;
When yet I had not walked above
A mile or two from my first love,
And looking back, at that short space,
10   Could see a glimpse of His bright face;
When on some gilded cloud or flower
My gazing soul would dwell an hour,
And in those weaker glories spy
Some shadows of eternity;
Before I taught my tongue to wound
My conscience with a sinful sound,
Or had the black art to dispense
A several sin to every sense,
But felt through all this fleshly dress
20   Bright shoots of everlastingness.
    O, how I long to travel back,
And tread again that ancient track!
That I might once more reach that plain
Where first I left my glorious train,
From whence th' enlightened spirit sees
That shady city of palm trees.
But, ah! my soul with too much stay
Is drunk, and staggers in the way.
Some men a forward motion love;
30   But I by backward steps would move,
And when this dust falls to the urn,
In that state I came, return.

(p. 245)

JONATHAN SWIFT (1667 – 1745)

A Description of the Morning

Now hardly here and there an hackney-coach
Appearing, showed the ruddy morn's approach.
Now Betty from her master's bed had flown,
And softly stole to discompose her own.
The slipshod 'prentice from his master's door,
Had pared the dirt, and sprinkled round the floor.
Now Moll had whirled her mop with dext'rous airs,
Prepared to scrub the entry and the stairs.
The youth with broomy stumps began to trace
10   The kennel edge, where wheels had worn the place.
The small-coal man was heard with cadence deep,
'Till drowned in shriller notes of chimney sweep,
Duns at his lordship's gate began to meet,
And brickdust Moll had screamed through half the street.
The turnkey now his flock returning sees,
Duly let out a-nights to steal for fees.
The watchful bailiffs take their silent stands;
And schoolboys lag with satchels in their hands.

(p. 245)

ALEXANDER POPE (1688–1744)

Epistle to Miss Blount
On her Leaving the Town after the Coronation

As some fond virgin, whom her mother's care
Drags from the town to wholsom country air,
Just when she learns to roll a melting eye,
And hear a spark, yet think no danger nigh;
From the dear man unwilling she must sever,
Yet takes one kiss before she departs for ever:
Thus from the world fair Zephalinda flew,
Saw others happy, and with sighs withdrew;
Not that their pleasures caus'd her discontent,
10   She sigh'd, not that they stay'd, but that she went.
    She went to plain-work, and to purling brooks,
Old-fashion'd halls, dull aunts, and croaking rooks,
She went from op'ra, park, assembly, play,
To morning walks, and pray'rs three hours a day;
To pass her time, 'twixt reading and bohea,
To muse, and spill her solitary tea,
Or o'er cold coffee trifle with the spoon,
Count the slow clock, and dine exact at noon;
Divert her eyes with pictures in the fire,
20   Hum half a tune, tell stories to the squire;
Up to her godly garret after sev'n,
There starve and pray, for that's the way to heav'n.
    Some Squire, perhaps, you take a delight to rack;
Whose game is whisk, whose treat a toast in sack,
Who visits with a gun, presents you birds,
Then gives a smacking buss, and cries—No words!
Or with his hound comes hollowing from the stable,
Makes love with nods, and knees beneath a table;
Whose laughs are hearty, tho' his jests are coarse,
30   And loves you best of all things—but his horse.
    In some fair evening, on your elbow laid,
You dream of triumphs in the rural shade;
In pensive thought recall the fancied scene,
See coronations rise on ev'ry green;
Before you pass th' imaginary sights
Of lords, and earls, and dukes, and garter'd knights;
While the spread fan o'ershades your closing eyes;

Then give one flirt, and all the vision flies.
Thus vanish sceptres, coronets and balls,
40 And leave you in lone woods, or empty walls.
  So when your slave, at some dear, idle time,
(Not plagu'd with headaches, or the want of rhyme)
Stands in the streets, abstracted from the crew,
And while he seems to study, thinks of you:
Just when his fancy points your sprightly eyes,
Or sees the blush of soft Parthenia rise,
Gay pats my shoulder, and you vanish quite;
Streets, chairs, and coxcombs rush upon my sight;
Vext to be still in town, I knit my brow,
50 Look sour, and hum a tune—as you may now.

(p. 245)

An Essay on Man (extract)

(Know then thyself . . .)

Know then thyself, presume not God to scan;
The proper study of Mankind is Man.
Plac'd on this isthmus of a middle state,
A being darkly wise, and rudely great:
With too much knowledge for the Sceptic side,
With too much weakness for the Stoic's pride,
He hangs between; in doubt to act, or rest,
In doubt to deem himself a God, or Beast;
In doubt his Mind or Body to prefer,
10 Born but to die, and reas'ning but to err;
Alike in ignorance, his reason such,
Whether he thinks too little, or too much:
Chaos of Thought and Passion, all confus'd;
Still by himself abus'd, or disabus'd;
Created half to rise, and half to fall;
Great lord of all things, yet a prey to all;
Sole judge of Truth, in endless Error hurl'd:
The glory, jest, and riddle of the world!

SAMUEL JOHNSON (1709—1784)

A Short Song of Congratulation

Long-expected one and twenty
    Lingering year at last is flown,
Pomp and Pleasure, Pride and Plenty,
    Great Sir John, are all your own.

Loosened from the minor's tether,
    Free to mortgage or to sell,
Wild as wind, and light as feather
    Bid the slaves of thrift farewell.

Call the Bettys, Kates, and Jennys
10   Every name that laughs at Care,
Lavish of your grandsire's guineas,
    Show the spirit of an heir.

All that prey on vice and folly
    Joy to see their quarry fly,
Here the gamester light and jolly
    There the lender grave and sly.

Wealth, Sir John, was made to wander,
    Let it wander as it will;
See the jockey, see the pander,
20   Bid them come, and take their fill.

When the bonny blade carouses,
    Pockets full, and spirits high,
What are acres? What are houses?
    Only dirt, or wet or dry.

If the guardian or the mother
    Tell the woes of wilful waste,
Scorn their counsel and their pother,
    You can hang or drown at last.

THOMAS GRAY (1716 – 1771)

Ode, On the Death of a Favourite Cat, Drowned in a Tub of Goldfishes

'Twas on a lofty vase's side,
Where China's gayest art had dyed
   The azure flowers that blow;
Demurest of the tabby kind,
The pensive Selima, reclined,
   Gazed on the lake below.

Her conscious tail her joy declared;
The fair round face, the snowy beard,
   The velvet of her paws,
10 Her coat, that with the tortoise vies,
Her ears of jet, and emerald eyes,
   She saw; and purred applause.

Still had she gazed; but 'midst the tide
Two angel forms were seen to glide,
   The genii of the stream:
Their scaly armour's Tyrian hue
Through richest purple to the view
   Betrayed a golden gleam.

The hapless nymph with wonder saw:
20 A whisker first and then a claw,
   With many an ardent wish,
She stretched in vain to reach the prize.
What female heart can gold despise?
   What cat's averse to fish?

Presumptuous maid! with looks intent
Again she stretched, again she bent,
   Nor knew the gulf between.
(Malignant Fate sat by and smiled)
The slippery verge her feet beguiled,
30   She tumbled headlong in.

Eight times emerging from the flood
She mewed to every watery god,
  Some speedy aid to send.
No dolphin came, no Nereid stirred;
Nor cruel Tom, nor Susan heard;
  A favourite has no friend!

From hence, ye beauties, undeceived,
Know, one false step is ne'er retrieved,
  And be with caution bold.
40 Not all that tempts your wandering eyes
And heedless hearts, is lawful prize;
  Nor all that glisters, gold.

(p. 245)

WILLIAM BLAKE (1757–1827)

from: *Songs of Innocence and Experience*
   'Showing the two contrary states of the human soul'

Nurse's Song

When the voices of children are heard on the green,
And laughing is heard on the hill,
My heart is at rest within my breast,
    And everything else is still.

'Then come home, my children, the sun is gone down,
And the dews of night arise;
Come, come, leave off play, and let us away
Till the morning appears in the skies.'

'No, no, let us play, for it is yet day,
And we cannot go to sleep;
Besides, in the sky the little birds fly
And the hills are all cover'd with sheep.'

'Well, well, go & play till the light fades away,
And then go home to bed.'
The little ones leaped & shouted & laugh'd
    And all the hills ecchoèd.

Nurse's Song

When the voices of children are heard on the green,
And whisp'rings are in the dale,
The days of my youth rise fresh in my mind,
My face turns green and pale.

Then come home, my children, the sun is gone down,
And the dews of night arise;
Your spring & your day are wasted in play,
And your winter and night in disguise.

(p. 246)

A Poison Tree

I was angry with my friend,
I told my wrath, my wrath did end;
I was angry with my foe,
I told it not, my wrath did grow.

And I water'd it in fears,
Night & morning with my tears;
And I sunned it with smiles,
And with soft deceitful wiles.

And it grew both day and night,
10   Till it bore an apple bright;
And my foe beheld it shine,
And he knew that it was mine,

And into my garden stole
When the night had veil'd the pole:
In the morning glad I see
My foe outstretch'd beneath the tree.

The Tyger

Tyger! Tyger! burning bright
In the forests of the night,
What immortal hand or eye
Could frame thy fearful symmetry?

In what distant deeps or skies
Burnt the fire of thine eyes?
On what wings dare he aspire?
What the hand dare seize the fire?

And what shoulder, & what art,
10   Could twist the sinews of thy heart?
And when thy heart began to beat,
What dread hand? & what dread feet?

What the hammer? what the chain?
In what furnace was thy brain?
What the anvil? what dread grasp
Dare its deadly terrors clasp?

When the stars threw down their spears,
And water'd heaven with their tears,
Did he smile his work to see?
20   Did he who made the Lamb make thee?

Tyger! Tyger! burning bright
In the forests of the night,
What immortal hand or eye
Dare frame thy fearful symmetry?

London

I wander thro' each charter'd street,
Near where the charter'd Thames does flow,
And mark in every face I meet
Marks of weakness, marks of woe.

In every cry of every Man,
In every Infant's cry of fear,
In every voice, in every ban,
The mind-forg'd manacles I hear.

How the Chimney-sweeper's cry
10   Every black'ning Church appalls,
And the hapless Soldier's sigh,
Runs in blood down Palace walls.

But most thro' midnight streets I hear
How the youthful Harlot's curse
Blasts the new-born Infant's tear
And blights with plagues the Marriage hearse.

ROBERT BURNS (1759 — 1796)

For A' That and A' That

Is there, for honest poverty,
    That hings his head, and a' that;
The coward-slave, we pass him by,
    We dare be poor for a' that!
        For a' that, and a' that,
            Our toils obscure, and a' that,
        The rank is but the guinea's stamp,
            The man's the gowd for a' that.

What though on hamely fare we dine,
10   Wear hoddin-grey, and a' that;
Gie fools their silks, and knaves their wine,
    A man's a man for a' that.
        For a' that, and a' that,
            Their tinsel show, and a' that;
        The honest man, tho' e'er sae poor,
            Is king o' men for a' that.

Ye see yon birkie, ca'd a lord,
    Wha struts, and stares, and a' that;
Tho' hundreds worship at his word,
20   He's but a coof for a' that.
        For a' that, and a' that,
            His ribband, star, and a' that,
        The man of independent mind,
            He looks and laughs at a' that.

A prince can mak a belted knight,
    A marquis, duke, and a' that;
But an honest man's aboon his might,
    Guid faith, he mauna fa' that!
        For a' that, and a' that,
30   Their dignities, and a' that,
        The pith o' sense, and pride o' worth,
            Are higher rank than a' that.

Then let us pray that come it may,
    As come it will for a' that,
That sense and worth, o'er a' the earth,
    Shall bear the gree, and a' that.
      For a' that and a' that,
        It's coming yet, for a' that,
      That man to man, the warld o'er,
40   Shall brothers be for a' that.

(p. 246)

O, my luve is like a red, red rose

O, my luve is like a red, red rose,
    That's newly sprung in June.
O, my luve is like the melodie,
    That's sweetly played in tune.

As fair art thou, my bonnie lass,
    So deep in luve am I,
And I will luve thee still, my dear,
    Till a' the seas gang dry.

Till a' the seas gang dry, my dear,
10   And the rocks melt wi' the sun!
And I will luve thee still, my dear,
    While the sands o' life shall run.

And fare thee weel, my only luve,
    And fare thee weel a while!
And I will come again, my luve,
    Though it were ten thousand mile!

WILLIAM WORDSWORTH (1770–1850)

There Was a Boy

There was a Boy; ye knew him well, ye cliffs
And islands of Winander!—many a time,
At evening, when the earliest stars began
To move along the edges of the hills,
Rising or setting, would he stand alone,
Beneath the trees, or by the glimmering lake;
And there, with fingers interwoven, both hands
Pressed closely palm to palm and to his mouth
Uplifted, he, as through an instrument,
10 Blew mimic hootings to the silent owls,
That they might answer him.—And they would shout
Across the watery vale, and shout again,
Responsive to his call,—with quivering peals,
and long halloos, and screams, and echoes loud
Redoubled and redoubled; concourse wild
Of jocund din! And, when there came a pause
Of silence such as baffled his best skill:
Then sometimes, in that silence, while he hung
Listening, a gentle shock of mild surprise
20 Has carried far into his heart the voice
Of mountain torrents; or the visible scene
Would enter unawares into his mind
With all its solemn imagery, its rocks,
Its woods, and that uncertain heaven received
Into the bosom of the steady lake.

This boy was taken from his mates, and died
In childhood, ere he was full twelve years old.
Pre-eminent in beauty is the vale
Where he was born and bred: the churchyard hangs
30 Upon a slope above the village-school;
And through that churchyard when my way has led
On summer-evenings, I believe that there
A long half-hour together I have stood
Mute—looking at the grave in which he lies!

Strange fits of passion have I known

Strange fits of passion have I known:
And I will dare to tell,
But in the Lover's ear alone,
What once to me befell.

When she I loved looked every day
Fresh as a rose in June,
I to her cottage bent my way,
Beneath an evening-moon.

Upon the moon I fixed my eye,
10 All over the wide lea;
With quickening pace my horse drew nigh
Those paths so dear to me.

And now we reached the orchard-plot;
And, as we climbed the hill,
The sinking moon to Lucy's cot
Came near, and nearer still.

In one of those sweet dreams I slept,
Kind Nature's gentlest boon!
And all the while my eyes I kept
20 On the descending moon.

My horse moved on; hoof after hoof
He raised, and never stopped:
When down behind the cottage roof,
At once, the bright moon dropped.

What fond and wayward thoughts will slide
Into a Lover's head!
'O mercy!' to myself I cried,
'If Lucy should be dead!'

(p. 246)

Lines Composed a Few Miles above Tintern Abbey
On Revisiting the Banks of the Wye During a Tour. July 13, 1798

Five years have passed; five summers, with the length
Of five long winters! And again I hear
These waters, rolling from their mountain-springs
With a soft inland murmur.—Once again
Do I behold these steep and lofty cliffs,
That on a wild secluded scene impress
Thoughts of more deep seclusion; and connect
The landscape with the quiet of the sky.
The day is come when I again repose
10   Here, under this dark sycamore, and view
These plots of cottage-ground, these orchard-tufts,
Which at this season, with their unripe fruits,
Are clad in one green hue, and lose themselves
'Mid groves and copses. Once again I see
These hedge-rows, hardly hedge-rows, little lines
Of sportive wood run wild: these pastoral farms,
Green to the very door; and wreaths of smoke
Sent up, in silence, from among the trees!
With some uncertain notice, as might seem
20   Of vagrant dwellers in the houseless woods,
Or of some Hermit's cave, where by his fire
The Hermit sits alone.

                These beauteous forms,
Through a long absence, have not been to me
As is a landscape to a blind man's eye:
But oft, in lonely rooms, and 'mid the din
Of towns and cities, I have owed to them
In hours of weariness, sensations sweet,
Felt in the blood, and felt along the heart;
And passing even into my purer mind,
30   With tranquil restoration:—feelings too
Of unremembered pleasure: such, perhaps,
As have no slight or trivial influence
On that best portion of a good man's life,
His little, nameless, unremembered, acts
Of kindness and of love. Nor less, I trust,
To them I may have owed another gift,
Of aspect more sublime; that blessed mood

In which the burthen of the mystery,
In which the heavy and the weary weight
40   Of all this unintelligible world,
Is lightened:—that serene and blessed mood
In which the affections gently lead us on,—
Until, the breath of this corporeal frame
And even the motion of our human blood
Almost suspended, we are laid asleep
In body, and become a living soul:
While with an eye made quiet by the power
Of harmony, and the deep power of joy,
We see into the life of things.
                    If this
50   Be but a vain belief, yet, oh! how oft—
In darkness and amid the many shapes
Of joyless daylight; when the fretful stir
Unprofitable, and the fever of the world,
Have hung upon the beatings of my heart—
How oft, in spirit, have I turned to thee,
O sylvan Wye! thou wanderer through the woods,
How often has my spirit turned to thee!

    And now, with gleams of half-extinguished thought,
With many recognitions dim and faint,
60   And somewhat of a sad perplexity,
The picture of the mind revives again:
While here I stand, not only with the sense
Of present pleasure, but with pleasing thoughts
That in this moment there is life and food
For future years. And so I dare to hope,
Though changed, no doubt, from what I was when first
I came among these hills; when like a roe
I bounded o'er the mountains, by the sides
Of the deep rivers, and the lonely streams,
70   Wherever nature led: more like a man
Flying from something that he dreads than one
Who sought the thing he loved. For nature then
(The coarser pleasures of my boyish days,
And their glad animal movements all gone by)
To me was all in all. —I cannot paint
What then I was. The sounding cataract

Haunted me like a passion: the tall rock,
The mountain, and the deep and gloomy wood,
Their colours and their forms, were then to me
80 An appetite; a feeling and a love,
That had no need of a remoter charm,
By thought supplied, nor any interest
Unborrowed from the eye.—That time is past,
And all its aching joys are now no more,
And all its dizzy raptures. Not for this
Faint I, nor mourn nor murmur; other gifts
Have followed; for such loss, I would believe,
Abundant recompense. For I have learned
To look on nature, not as in the hour
90 Of thoughtless youth; but hearing oftentimes
The still, sad music of humanity,
Nor harsh nor grating, though of ample power
To chasten and subdue. And I have felt
A presence that disturbs me with the joy
Of elevated thoughts; a sense sublime
Of something far more deeply interfused,
Whose dwelling is the light of setting suns,
And the round ocean and the living air,
And the blue sky, and in the mind of man:
100 A motion and a spirit, that impels
All thinking things, all objects of all thought,
And rolls through all things. Therefore am I still
A lover of the meadows and the woods,
And mountains; and of all that we behold
From this green earth; of all the mighty world
Of eye, and ear,—both what they half create,
And what perceive; well pleased to recognize
In nature and the language of the sense
The anchor of my purest thoughts, the nurse,
110 The guide, the guardian of my heart, and soul
Of all my moral being.
                              Nor perchance,
If I were not thus taught, should I the more
Suffer my genial spirits to decay:
For thou art with me here upon the banks
Of this fair river; thou my dearest Friend,
My dear, dear Friend; and in thy voice I catch

The language of my former heart, and read
My former pleasures in the shooting lights
Of thy wild eyes. Oh! yet a little while
120 May I behold in thee what I was once,
My dear, dear Sister! and this prayer I make,
Knowing that Nature never did betray
The heart that loved her; 'tis her privilege,
Through all the years of this our life, to lead
From joy to joy: for she can so inform
The mind that is within us, so impress
With quietness and beauty, and so feed
With lofty thoughts, that neither evil tongues,
Rash judgements, nor the sneers of selfish men,
130 Nor greetings where no kindness is, nor all
The dreary intercourse of daily life,
Shall e'er prevail against us, or disturb
Our cheerful faith, that all which we behold
Is full of blessings. Therefore let the moon
Shine on thee in thy solitary walk;
And let the misty mountain-winds be free
To blow against thee: and, in after years,
When these wild ecstasies shall be matured
Into a sober pleasure; when thy mind
140 Shall be a mansion for all lovely forms,
Thy memory be as a dwelling-place
For all sweet sounds and harmonies; oh! then,
If solitude, or fear, or pain, or grief,
Should be thy portion, with what healing thoughts
Of tender joy wilt thou remember me,
And these my exhortations! Nor, perchance—
If I should be where I no more can hear
Thy voice, nor catch from thy wild eyes these gleams
Of past existence—wilt thou then forget
150 That on the banks of this delightful stream
We stood together; and that I, so long
A worshipper of Nature, hither came

Unwearied in that service: rather say
With warmer love—oh! with far deeper zeal
Of holier love. Nor wilt thou then forget,
That after many wanderings, many years
Of absence, these steep woods and lofty cliffs,
And this green pastoral landscape, were to me
More dear, both for themselves and for thy sake!

(p. 246)

Composed upon Westminster Bridge, September 3, 1802

Earth has not anything to show more fair:
Dull would he be of soul who could pass by
A sight so touching in its majesty:
This City now doth, like a garment, wear
The beauty of the morning; silent, bare,
Ships, towers, domes, theatres, and temples lie
Open unto the fields, and to the sky;
All bright and glittering in the smokeless air.
Never did sun more beautifully steep
10 In his first splendour, valley, rock, or hill;
Ne'er saw I, never felt, a calm so deep!
The river glideth at his own sweet will;
Dear God! the very houses seem asleep;
And all that mighty heart is lying still!

SAMUEL TAYLOR COLERIDGE (1772–1834)

Frost at Midnight

The Frost performs its secret ministry,
Unhelped by any wind. The owlet's cry
Came loud—and hark, again! loud as before.
The inmates of my cottage, all at rest,
Have left me to that solitude, which suits
Abstruser musings: save that at my side
My cradled infant slumbers peacefully.
'Tis calm indeed! so calm, that it disturbs
And vexes meditation with its strange

10 And extreme silentness. Sea, hill, and wood,
This populous village! Sea, and hill, and wood,
With all the numberless goings-on of life,
Inaudible as dreams! the thin blue flame
Lies on my low-burnt fire, and quivers not;
Only that film, which fluttered on the grate,
Still flutters there, the sole unquiet thing.
Methinks, its motion in this hush of nature
Gives it dim sympathies with me who live,
Making it a companionable form,

20 Whose puny flaps and freaks the idling Spirit
By its own mood interprets, everywhere
Echo or mirror seeking of itself,
And makes a toy of Thought.
                      But O! how oft,
How oft, at school, with most believing mind,
Presageful, have I gazed upon the bars,
To watch that fluttering *stranger!* and as oft
With unclosed lids, already had I dreamt
Of my sweet birth-place, and the old church-tower,
Whose bells, the poor man's only music, rang

30 From morn to evening, all the hot Fair-day,
So sweetly, that they stirred and haunted me
With a wild pleasure, falling on mine ear
Most like articulate sounds of things to come!
So gazed I, till the soothing things, I dreamt,
Lulled me to sleep, and sleep prolonged my dreams!
And so I brooded all the following morn,

Awed by the stern preceptor's face, mine eye
Fixed with mock study on my swimming book:
Save if the door half opened, and I snatched
40   A hasty glance, and still my heart leaped up,
For still I hoped to see the *stranger's* face,
Townsman, or aunt, or sister more beloved,
My play-mate when we both were clothed alike!

Dear Babe, that sleepest cradled by my side,
Whose gentle breathings, heard in this deep calm,
Fill up the interspersèd vacancies
And momentary pauses of the thought!
My babe so beautiful! it thrills my heart
With tender gladness, thus to look at thee,
50   And think that thou shalt learn far other lore,
And in far other scenes! For I was reared
In the great city, pent 'mid cloisters dim,
And saw nought lovely but the sky and stars.
But *thou*, my babe! shalt wander like a breeze
By lakes and sandy shores, beneath the crags
Of ancient mountain, and beneath the clouds,
Which image in their bulk both lakes and shores
And mountain crags: so shalt thou see and hear
The lovely shapes and sounds intelligible
60   Of that eternal language, which thy God
Utters, who from eternity doth teach
Himself in all, and all things in himself.
Great universal Teacher! he shall mould
Thy spirit, and by giving make it ask.

Therefore all seasons shall be sweet to thee,
Whether the summer clothe the general earth
With greenness, or the redbreast sit and sing
Betwixt the tufts of snow on the bare branch
Of mossy apple-tree, while the nigh thatch
70   Smokes in the sun-thaw; whether the eave-drops fall
Heard only in the trances of the blast,
Or if the secret ministry of frost
Shall hang them up in silent icicles,
Quietly shining to the quiet Moon.

(p. 246)

Kubla Khan
Or, A Vision in a Dream. A Fragment.

In Xanadu did Kubla Khan
A stately pleasure-dome decree:
Where Alph, the sacred river, ran
Through caverns measureless to man
    Down to a sunless sea.
So twice five miles of fertile ground
With walls and towers were girdled round:
And there were gardens bright with sinuous rills,
Where blossomed many an incense-bearing tree;
10 And here were forests ancient as the hills,
Enfolding sunny spots of greenery.

But oh! that deep romantic chasm which slanted
Down the green hill athwart a cedarn cover!
A savage place! as holy and enchanted
As e'er beneath a waning moon was haunted
By woman wailing for her demon-lover!
And from this chasm, with ceaseless turmoil seething,
As if this earth in fast thick pants were breathing,
A mighty fountain momently was forced:
20 Amid whose swift half-intermitted burst
Huge fragments vaulted like rebounding hail,
Or chaffy grain beneath the thresher's flail:
And 'mid these dancing rocks at once and ever
It flung up momently the sacred river.
Five miles meandering with a mazy motion
Through wood and dale the sacred river ran,
Then reached the caverns measureless to man,
And sank in tumult to a lifeless ocean:
And 'mid this tumult Kubla heard from far
30 Ancestral voices prophesying war!
    The shadow of the dome of pleasure
    Floated midway on the waves;
    Where was heard the mingled measure
    From the fountain and the caves.
It was a miracle of rare device,
A sunny pleasure-dome with caves of ice!

A damsel with a dulcimer
In a vision once I saw:
It was an Abyssinian maid,
40   And on her dulcimer she played,
Singing of Mount Abora.
Could I revive within me
Her symphony and song,
To such a deep delight 'twould win me,
That with music loud and long,
I would build that dome in air,
That sunny dome! those caves of ice!
And all who heard should see them there,
And all should cry, Beware! Beware!
50   His flashing eyes, his floating hair!
Weave a circle round him thrice,
And close your eyes with holy dread,
For he on honey-dew hath fed,
And drunk the milk of Paradise.

(p. 246)

GEORGE GORDON, LORD BYRON (1788–1824)

Sonnet on Chillon

Eternal Spirit of the chainless Mind!
    Brightest in dungeons, Liberty! thou art,
    For there thy habitation is the heart—
The heart which love of thee alone can bind;
And when thy sons to fetters are consign'd—
    To fetters, and the damp vault's dayless gloom,
    Their country conquers with their martyrdom,
And Freedom's fame finds wings on every wind.
Chillon! thy prison is a holy place,
10   And thy sad floor an altar—for 'twas trod,
Until his very steps have left a trace
    Worn, as if thy cold pavement were a sod,
By Bonnivard!—May none those marks efface!
    For they appeal from tyranny to God.

(p. 246)

from: Beppo

'England! with all thy faults I love thee still,'
    I said at Calais, and have not forgot it;
I like to speak and lucubrate my fill;
    I like the government (but that is not it);
I like the freedom of the press and quill;
    I like the Habeas Corpus (when we've got it);
I like a parliamentary debate,
Particularly when 'tis not too late;

I like the taxes, when they're not too many;
10   I like a seacoal fire, when not too dear;
I like a beef-steak, too, as well as any;
    Have no objection to a pot of beer;
I like the weather, when it is not rainy,
    That is, I like two months of every year,
And so God save the Regent, Church, and King!
Which means that I like all and everything.

Our standing army, and disbanded seamen,
 Poor's rate, Reform, my own, the nation's debt,
Our little riots just to show we are free men,
 Our trifling bankruptcies in the *Gazette*,
Our cloudy climate, and our chilly women,
 All these I can forgive, and those forget,
And greatly venerate our recent glories,
And wish they were not owing to the Tories.

(XLVII–XLIX)

(p. 246)

3

PERCY BYSSHE SHELLEY (1792–1822)

Ozymandias

I met a traveller from an antique land
Who said: Two vast and trunkless legs of stone
Stand in the desert . . . Near them, on the sand,
Half sunk, a shattered visage lies, whose frown,
And wrinkled lip, and sneer of cold command,
Tell that its sculptor well those passions read
Which yet survive, stamped on these lifeless things,
The hand that mocked them, and the heart that fed:
And on the pedestal these words appear:
10 'My name is Ozymandias, king of kings:
Look on my works, ye Mighty, and despair!'
Nothing beside remains. Round the decay
Of that colossal wreck, boundless and bare
The lone and level sands stretch far away.

England in 1819

An old, mad, blind, despised, and dying king,—
Princes, the dregs of their dull race, who flow
Through public scorn,—mud from a muddy spring,—
Rulers who neither see, nor feel, nor know,
But leech-like to their fainting country cling,
Till they drop, blind in blood, without a blow,—
A people starved and stabbed in the untilled field,—
An army, which liberticide and prey
Makes as a two-edged sword to all who wield,—
10 Golden and sanguine laws which tempt and slay;
Religion Christless, Godless—a book sealed;
A Senate,—Time's worst statute unrepealed,—
Are graves, from which a glorious Phantom may
Burst, to illuminate our tempestuous day.

(p. 247)

94

Ode to the West Wind

1

O wild West Wind, thou breath of Autumn's being,
Thou, from whose unseen presence the leaves dead
Are driven, like ghosts from an enchanter fleeing,

Yellow, and black, and pale, and hectic red,
Pestilence-stricken multitudes: O thou,
Who chariotest to their dark wintry bed

The wingèd seeds, where they lie cold and low,
Each like a corpse within its grave, until
Thine azure sister of the Spring shall blow

10   Her clarion o'er the dreaming earth, and fill
(Driving sweet buds like flocks to feed in air)
With living hues and odours plain and hill:

Wild Spirit, which art moving everywhere;
Destroyer and preserver; hear, oh, hear!

2

Thou on whose stream, 'mid the steep sky's commotion,
Loose clouds like earth's decaying leaves are shed,
Shook from the tangled boughs of Heaven and Ocean,

Angels of rain and lightning: there are spread
On the blue surface of thine aëry surge,
20   Like the bright hair uplifted from the head

Of some fierce Maenad, even from the dim verge
Of the horizon to the zenith's height,
The locks of the approaching storm. Thou dirge

Of the dying year, to which this closing night
Will be the dome of a vast sepulchre,
Vaulted with all thy congregated might

Of vapours, from whose solid atmosphere
Black rain, and fire, and hail will burst: oh, hear!

3

Thou who didst waken from his summer dreams
30 The blue Mediterranean, where he lay,
Lulled by the coil of his crystalline streams,

Beside a pumice isle in Baiae's bay,
And saw in sleep old palaces and towers
Quivering within the wave's intenser day,

All overgrown with azure moss and flowers
So sweet, the sense faints picturing them! Thou
For whose path the Atlantic's level powers

Cleave themselves into chasms, while far below
The sea-blooms and the oozy woods which wear
40 The sapless foliage of the ocean, know

Thy voice, and suddenly grow gray with fear,
And tremble and despoil themselves: oh, hear!

4

If I were a dead leaf thou mightest bear;
If I were a swift cloud to fly with thee;
A wave to pant beneath thy power, and share

The impulse of thy strength, only less free
Than thou, O uncontrollable! If even
I were as in my boyhood, and could be

The comrade of thy wanderings over Heaven,
50 As then, when to outstrip thy skiey speed
Scarce seemed a vision; I would ne'er have striven

As thus with thee in prayer in my sore need.
Oh, lift me as a wave, a leaf, a cloud!
I fall upon the thorns of life! I bleed!

A heavy weight of hours has chained and bowed
One too like thee: tameless, and swift, and proud.

Make me thy lyre, even as the forest is:
What if my leaves are falling like its own!
The tumult of thy mighty harmonies

0   Will take from both a deep, autumnal tone,
Sweet though in sadness. Be thou, Spirit fierce,
My spirit! Be thou me, impetuous one!

Drive my dead thoughts over the universe
Like withered leaves to quicken a new birth!
And, by the incantation of this verse,

Scatter, as from an unextinguished hearth
Ashes and sparks, my words among mankind!
Be through my lips to unawakened earth

70 The trumpet of a prophecy! O, Wind,
If Winter comes, can Spring be far behind?

(p. 247)

JOHN CLARE (1793–1864)

First Love

I ne'er was struck before that hour
    With love so sudden and so sweet,
Her face it bloomed like a sweet flower
    And stole my heart away complete.
My face turned pale as deadly pale,
    My legs refused to walk away,
And when she looked, what could I ail?
    My life and all seemed turned to clay.

And then my blood rushed to my face
10   And took my eyesight quite away,
The trees and bushes round the place
    Seemed midnight at noonday.
I could not see a single thing,
    Words from my eyes did start—
They spoke as chords do from the string,
    And blood burnt round my heart.

Are flowers the winter's choice?
    Is love's bed always snow?
She seemed to hear my silent voice,
20   Not love's appeals to know.
I never saw so sweet a face
    As that I stood before.
My heart has left its dwelling place
    And can return no more.

JOHN KEATS (1795–1821)

Bright Star

Bright star, would I were steadfast as thou art—
 Not in lone splendour hung aloft the night
And watching, with eternal lids apart,
 Like nature's patient, sleepless Eremite,
The moving waters at their priestlike task
 Of pure ablution round earth's human shores,
Or gazing on the new soft-fallen mask
 Of snow upon the mountains and the moors—
No—yet still steadfast, still unchangeable,
 Pillow'd upon my fair love's ripening breast,
To feel for ever its soft fall and swell,
 Awake for ever in a sweet unrest,
Still, still to hear her tender-taken breath,
And so live ever—or else swoon to death.

(p. 247)

When I have fears that I may cease to be

When I have fears that I may cease to be
 Before my pen has glean'd my teeming brain,
Before high-piled books, in charactery,
 Hold like rich garners the full ripen'd grain;
When I behold, upon the night's starr'd face,
 Huge cloudy symbols of a high romance,
And think that I may never live to trace
 Their shadows with the magic hand of chance;
And when I feel, fair creature of an hour,
 That I shall never look upon thee more,
Never have relish in the faery power
 Of unreflecting love;—then on the shore
Of the wide world I stand alone, and think
Till love and fame to nothingness do sink.

p. 247)

To Autumn

1

Season of mists and mellow fruitfulness,
    Close bosom-friend of the maturing sun;
Conspiring with him how to load and bless
    With fruit the vines that round the thatch-eves run;
To bend with apples the moss'd cottage-trees,
    And fill all fruit with ripeness to the core;
        To swell the gourd, and plump the hazel shells
With a sweet kernel; to set budding more,
    And still more, later flowers for the bees,
10   Until they think warm days will never cease,
        For Summer has o'er-brimm'd their clammy cells.

2

Who hath not seen thee oft amid thy store?
    Sometimes whoever seeks abroad may find
Thee sitting careless on a granary floor,
    Thy hair soft-lifted by the winnowing wind;
Or on a half-reap'd furrow sound asleep,
    Drows'd with the fume of poppies, while thy hook
        Spares the next swath and all its twinèd flowers:
And sometimes like a gleaner thou dost keep
20   Steady thy laden head across a brook;
    Or by a cyder-press, with patient look,
        Thou watchest the last oozings hours by hours.

3

Where are the songs of Spring? Ay, where are they?
    Think not of them, thou hast thy music too, —
While barred clouds bloom the soft-dying day,
    And touch the stubble-plains with rosy hue;
Then in a wailful choir the small gnats mourn
    Among the river sallows, borne aloft
        Or sinking as the light wind lives or dies;
30   And full-grown lambs loud bleat from hilly bourn;
    Hedge-crickets sing; and now with treble soft
    The red-breast whistles from a garden-croft;
        And gathering swallows twitter in the skies.

(p. 247)

THOMAS PRINGLE (1789–1834)

Afar in the Desert

Afar in the Desert I love to ride,
With the silent Bush-boy alone by my side:
When the sorrows of life the soul o'ercast,
And, sick of the Present, I cling to the Past;
When the eye is suffused with regretful tears,
From the fond recollections of former years;
And shadows of things that have long since fled
Flit over the brain, like the ghosts of the dead:
Bright visions of glory—that vanished too soon;
10   Day-dreams—that departed ere manhood's noon;
Attachments—by fate or by falsehood reft;
Companions of early days—lost or left;
And my Native Land—whose magical name
Thrills to the heart like electric flame;
The home of my childhood; the haunts of my prime;
All the passions and scenes of that rapturous time
When the feelings were young and the world was new,
Like the fresh bowers of Eden unfolding to view;
All—all now forsaken—forgotten—foregone!
20   And I—a lone exile remembered of none—
My high aims abandoned,—my good acts undone,—
Aweary of all that is under the sun,—
With that sadness of heart which no stranger may scan,
I fly to the Desert afar from man!

Afar in the Desert I love to ride,
With the silent Bush-boy alone by my side:
When the wild turmoil of this wearisome life,
With its scenes of oppression, corruption, and strife—
The proud man's frown, and the base man's fear,—
30   The scorner's laugh, and the sufferer's tear,—
And malice, and meanness, and falsehood, and folly,
Dispose me to musing and dark melancholy;
When my bosom is full, and my thoughts are high,
And my soul is sick with the bondman's sigh—
Oh! then there is freedom, and joy, and pride,
Afar in the Desert alone to ride!

There is rapture to vault on the champing steed,
And to bound away with the eagle's speed,
With the death-fraught firelock in my hand—
40   The only law of the Desert Land!

    Afar in the Desert I love to ride,
With the silent Bush-boy alone by my side:
Away—away from the dwellings of men,
By the wild deer's haunt, by the buffalo's glen;
By valleys remote where the oribi plays,
Where the gnu, the gazelle, and the hartebeest graze,
And the kudu and eland unhunted recline
By the skirts of grey forests o'erhung with wild-vine;
Where the elephant browses at peace in his wood,
50   And the river-horse gambols unscared in the flood,
And the mighty rhinoceros wallows at will
In the fen where the wild-ass is drinking his fill.

    Afar in the Desert I love to ride,
With the silent Bush-boy alone by my side:
O'er the brown Karroo, where the bleating cry
Of the springbok's fawn sounds plaintively;
And the timorous quagga's shrill whistling neigh
Is heard by the fountain at twilight grey;
Where the zebra wantonly tosses his mane,
60   With wild hoof scouring the desolate plain;
And the fleet-footed ostrich over the waste
Speeds like a horseman who travels in haste,
Hying away to the home of her rest,
Where she and her mate have scooped their nest,
Far hid from the pitiless plunderer's view
In the pathless depths of the parched Karroo.

    Afar in the Desert I love to ride,
With the silent Bush-boy alone by my side:
Away—away—in the Wilderness vast,
70   Where the White Man's foot hath never passed,
And the quivered Coránna or Bechuán
Hath rarely crossed with his roving clan:
A region of emptiness, howling and drear,
Which Man hath abandoned from famine and fear;
Which the snake and the lizard inhabit alone,

With the twilight bat from the yawning stone;
Where grass, nor herb, nor shrub takes root,
Save poisonous thorns that pierce the foot;
And the bitter-melon, for food and drink,
80 Is the pilgrim's fare by the salt lake's brink:
A region of drought, where no river glides,
Nor rippling brook with osiered sides;
Where sedgy pool, nor bubbling fount,
Nor tree, nor cloud, nor misty mount,
Appears, to refresh the aching eye:
But the barren earth, and the burning sky,
And the blank horizon, round and round,
Spread—void of living sight or sound.

    And here, while the night-winds round me sigh,
90 And the stars burn bright in the midnight sky,
As I sit apart by the desert stone,
Like Elijah at Horeb's cave alone,
'A still small voice' comes through the wild
(Like a Father consoling his fretful Child),
Which banishes bitterness, wrath, and fear,—
Saying—MAN IS DISTANT, BUT GOD IS NEAR!

(p. 247)

Makanna's Gathering

Wake! Amakósa, wake!
    And arm yourselves for war.
As coming winds the forest shake,
    I hear a sound from far:
It is not thunder in the sky,
    Nor lion's roar upon the hill,
But the voice of Him who sits on high,
    And bids me speak his will!

He bids me call you forth,
10   Bold sons of Káhabee,
To sweep the White Men from the earth,
    And drive them to the sea:

The sea, which heaved them up at first,
    For Amakósa's curse and bane,
Howls for the progeny she nurst,
    To swallow them again.

Hark! 'tis Uhlanga's voice
    From Debè's mountain caves!
He calls you now to make your choice—
20   To conquer or be slaves:
To meet proud Amanglézi's guns,
    And fight like warriors nobly born:
Or, like Umláo's feeble sons,
    Become the freeman's scorn.

Then come, ye Chieftains bold,
    With war-plumes waving high;
Come, every warrior young and old,
    With club and assegai.
Remember how the spoiler's host
30   Did through our land like locusts range!
Your herds, your wives, your comrades lost—
    Remember—and revenge!

Fling your broad shields away—
    Bootless against such foes;
But hand to hand we'll fight today,
    And with their bayonets close.
Grasp each man short his stabbing spear—
    And, when to battle's edge we come,
Rush on their ranks in full career,
40   And to their hearts strike home!

Wake! Amakósa, wake!
    And muster for the war:
The wizard-wolves from Keisi's brake,
    The vultures from afar,
Are gathering at Uhlanga's call,
    And follow fast our westward way—
For well they know, ere evening-fall,
    They shall have glorious prey!

(p. 247)

FREDERIC BROOKS (dates unknown)

Nature's Logic; or, Isaak van Batavia's Plea for his Manhood.
A True Story

Question.
Where do you live my Slave Boy, say?
I want to hire you by the day.

Answer.
Massa me no Slave *Boy* be;
Me be free *Man*, me be free.

Question.
Who gave you your freedom my black *boy*?
Will you not come to my employ?

Answer.
Yes *Massa*, me come, do every *ting*,
My hands, and feet, and heart, me bring;
But, when me come to your employ,
10   Me be a *Man*, me be no *Boy*.

Question.
A *Man!!!* a *Man!!!* who tells you so?
How far does his knowledge go;– *(aside)*
Who gave you thoughts above your station,
To unfit you for your avocation?

Answer.
Massa, the Great Big Book did say,
When God from darkness made the day;
And Sun, and Moon, and Stars, so high,
Like twinkling diamonds in the sky;
That, by and by, by His own plan,
20   He spake to *dust*, and up rose *Man*.
Adam *my father* was, and *thine*,
O! let I pray your heart incline,
Without a wrangle and no bother,
To hail *me* as a *Man* and *Brother*.

For fleecy locks and black complexion
    Cannot alter nature's claim;
Skins may differ, but affection
    Dwells in *Black* and *White* the same.

(p. 248)

105

ALFRED, LORD TENNYSON (1809–1892)

from: *In Memoriam A.H.H.*

Old Yew, which graspest at the stones

Old Yew, which graspest at the stones
    That name the under-lying dead,
    Thy fibres net the dreamless head,
Thy roots are wrapt about the bones.

The seasons bring the flower again,
    And bring the firstling to the flock;
    And in the dusk of thee, the clock
Beats out the little lives of men.

O not for thee the glow, the bloom,
    Who changest not in any gale,
    Nor branding summer suns avail
To touch thy thousand years of gloom:

And gazing on thee, sullen tree,
    Sick for thy stubborn hardihood,
    I seem to fail from out my blood
And grow incorporate into thee.

Dark house, by which once more I stand

Dark house, by which once more I stand
    Here in the long unlovely street,
    Doors, where my heart was used to beat
So quickly, waiting for a hand,

A hand that can be clasp'd no more—
    Behold me, for I cannot sleep,
    And like a guilty thing I creep
At earliest morning to the door.

He is not here; but far away
10   The noise of life begins again,
    And ghastly thro' the drizzling rain
On the bald street breaks the blank day.

Now fades the last long streak of snow

Now fades the last long streak of snow,
    Now burgeons every maze of quick
    About the flowering squares, and thick
By ashen roots the violets blow.

Now rings the woodland loud and long,
    The distance takes a lovelier hue,
    And drown'd in yonder living blue
The lark becomes a sightless song.

Now dance the lights on lawn and lea,
10   The flocks are whiter down the vale,
    And milkier every milky sail
On winding stream or distant sea;

Where now the seamew pipes, or dives
    In yonder greening gleam, and fly
    The happy birds, that change their sky
To build and brood; that live their lives

From land to land; and in my breast
    Spring wakens too; and my regret
    Becomes an April violet,
20 And buds and blossoms like the rest.

Doors, where my heart was used to beat

Doors, where my heart was used to beat
    So quickly, not as one that weeps
    I come once more; the city sleeps;
I smell the meadow in the street;

I hear a chirp of birds; I see
    Betwixt the black fronts long-withdrawn
    A light-blue lane of early dawn,
And think of early days and thee,

And bless thee, for thy lips are bland
10   And bright the friendship of thine eye;
    And in my thoughts with scarce a sigh
I take the pressure of thine hand.

Ulysses

It little profits that an idle king,
By this still hearth, among these barren crags,
Matched with an aged wife, I mete and dole
Unequal laws unto a savage race,
That hoard, and sleep, and feed, and know not me.
I cannot rest from travel: I will drink
Life to the lees: all times I have enjoyed
Greatly, have suffered greatly, both with those
That loved me, and alone; on shore, and when
10 Through scudding drifts the rainy Hyades
Vexed the dim sea: I am become a name;
For always roaming with a hungry heart
Much have I seen and known; cities of men
And manners, climates, councils, governments,
Myself not least, but honoured of them all;
And drunk delight of battle with my peers,
Far on the ringing plains of windy Troy.
I am a part of all that I have met;
Yet all experience is an arch wherethrough
20 Gleams that untravelled world, whose margin fades
For ever and for ever when I move.
How dull it is to pause, to make an end,
To rust unburnished, not to shine in use!
As though to breathe were life. Life piled on life
Were all too little, and of one to me
Little remains: but every hour is saved
From that eternal silence, something more,
A bringer of new things; and vile it were
For some three suns to store and hoard myself,

30   And this gray spirit yearning in desire
       To follow knowledge like a sinking star,
       Beyond the utmost bound of human thought.

           This is my son, mine own Telemachus,
       To whom I leave the sceptre and the isle—
       Well-loved of me, discerning to fulfil
       This labour, by slow prudence to make mild
       A rugged people, and through soft degrees
       Subdue them to the useful and the good.
       Most blameless is he, centred in the sphere
40   Of common duties, decent not to fail
       In offices of tenderness, and pay
       Meet adoration to my household gods,
       When I am gone. He works his work, I mine.

           There lies the port; the vessel puffs her sail:
       There gloom the dark broad seas. My mariners,
       Souls that have toiled, and wrought, and thought with me—
       That ever with a frolic welcome took
       The thunder and the sunshine, and opposed
       Free hearts, free foreheads—you and I are old;
50   Old age hath yet his honour and his toil;
       Death closes all: but something ere the end,
       Some work of noble note, may yet be done,
       Not unbecoming men that strove with Gods.
       The lights begin to twinkle from the rocks:
       The long day wanes: the slow moon climbs: the deep
       Moans round with many voices. Come, my friends,
       'Tis not too late to seek a newer world.
       Push off, and sitting well in order smite
       The sounding furrows; for my purpose holds
60   To sail beyond the sunset, and the baths
       Of all the western stars, until I die.
       It may be that the gulfs will wash us down:
       It may be we shall touch the Happy Isles,
       And see the great Achilles, whom we knew.
       Though much is taken, much abides; and though
       We are not now that strength which in old days
       Moved earth and heaven; that which we are, we are;
       One equal temper of heroic hearts,
       Made weak by time and fate, but strong in will
70   To strive, to seek, to find, and not to yield.

(p. 248)

ROBERT BROWNING (1812–1889)

My Last Duchess
Ferrara

That's my last Duchess painted on the wall,
Looking as if she were alive. I call
That piece a wonder, now: Frà Pandolf's hands
Worked busily a day, and there she stands.
Will't please you sit and look at her? I said
'Frà Pandolf' by design, for never read
Strangers like you that pictured countenance,
The depth and passion of its earnest glance,
But to myself they turned (since none puts by
10   The curtain I have drawn for you, but I)
And seemed as they would ask me, if they durst,
How such a glance came there; so, not the first
Are you to turn and ask thus. Sir, 't was not
Her husband's presence only, called that spot
Of joy into the Duchess' cheek: perhaps
Frà Pandolf chanced to say 'Her mantle laps
Over my lady's wrist too much,' or 'Paint
Must never hope to reproduce the faint
Half-flush that dies along her throat': such stuff
20   Was courtesy, she thought, and cause enough
For calling up that spot of joy. She had
A heart—how shall I say?— too soon made glad,
Too easily impressed; she liked whate'er
She looked on, and her looks went everywhere.
Sir, 't was all one! My favour at her breast,
The dropping of the daylight in the West,
The bough of cherries some officious fool
Broke in the orchard for her, the white mule
She rode with round the terrace—all and each
30   Would draw from her alike the approving speech,
Or blush, at least. She thanked men,—good! but thanked
Somehow—I know not how—as if she ranked
My gift of a nine-hundred-years-old name
With anybody's gift. Who'd stoop to blame
This sort of trifling? Even had you skill
In speech—(which I have not)—to make your will

Quite clear to such an one, and say, 'Just this
Or that in you disgusts me; here you miss,
Or there exceed the mark'—and if she let
40 Herself be lessoned so, nor plainly set
Her wits to yours, forsooth, and made excuse,
  —E'en then would be some stooping; and I choose
Never to stoop. Oh sir, she smiled, no doubt,
Whene'er I passed her; but who passed without
Much the same smile? This grew; I gave commands;
Then all smiles stopped together. There she stands
As if alive. Will't please you rise? We'll meet
The company below, then I repeat,
The Count your master's known munificence
50 Is ample warrant that no just pretence
Of mine for dowry will be disallowed;
Though his fair daughter's self, as I avowed
At starting, is my object. Nay, we'll go
Together down, sir. Notice Neptune, though,
Taming a sea-horse, thought a rarity,
Which Claus of Innsbruck cast in bronze for me!

(p. 248)

WALT WHITMAN (1819–1892)

Cavalry Crossing a Ford

A line in long array, where they wind betwixt green islands;
They take a serpentine course—their arms flash in the sun—Hark
    to the musical clank;
Behold the silvery river—in it the splashing horses, loitering, stop
    to drink;
Behold the brown-faced men—each group, each person, a picture
    —the negligent rest on the saddles;
Some emerge on the opposite bank—others are just entering the
    ford—while,
Scarlet, and blue, and snowy white,
The guidon flags flutter gaily in the wind.

(p. 248)

Sparkles from the Wheel

Where the city's ceaseless crowd moves on the livelong day,
Withdrawn I join a group of children watching, I pause aside with
    them.
By the curb toward the edge of the flagging,
A knife-grinder works at his wheel sharpening a great knife,
Bending over he carefully holds it to the stone, by foot and knee,
With measured tread he turns rapidly, as he presses with light but
    firm hand,
Forth issue then in copious golden jets,
Sparkles from the wheel.

The scene and all its belongings, how they seize and affect me,
10 The sad sharp-chinned old man with worn clothes and broad
    shoulder-band of leather,
Myself effusing and fluid, a phantom curiously floating, now here
    absorbed and arrested,
The group (an unminded point set in a vast surrounding),
The attentive, quiet children, the loud, proud, restive base of the
    streets,
The low hoarse purr of the whirling stone, the light-pressed blade,
Diffusing, dropping, sideways-darting, in tiny showers of gold,
Sparkles from the wheel.

MATTHEW ARNOLD (1822-1888)

Dover Beach

The sea is calm tonight.
The tide is full, the moon lies fair
Upon the straits—on the French coast the light
Gleams and is gone; the cliffs of England stand,
Glimmering and vast, out in the tranquil bay.
Come to the window, sweet is the night air!
Only, from the long line of spray
Where the sea meets the moon-blanched land,
Listen! you hear the grating roar
10   Of pebbles which the waves draw back, and fling,
At their return, up the high strand,
Begin, and cease, and then again begin,
With tremulous cadence slow, and bring
The eternal note of sadness in.

Sophocles long ago
Heard it on the Aegean, and it brought
Into his mind the turbid ebb and flow
Of human misery; we
Find also in the sound a thought,
20   Hearing it by this distant northern sea.

The Sea of Faith
Was once, too, at the full, and round earth's shore
Lay like the folds of a bright girdle furled.
But now I only hear
Its melancholy, long, withdrawing roar,
Retreating, to the breath
Of the night wind, down the vast edges drear
And naked shingles of the world.

Ah, love, let us be true
30   To one another! for the world, which seems
To lie before us like a land of dreams,
So various, so beautiful, so new,

Hath really neither joy, nor love, nor light,
Nor certitude, nor peace, nor help for pain;
And we are here as on a darkling plain
Swept with confused alarms of struggle and flight,
Where ignorant armies clash by night.

(p. 248)

On the Rhine

Vain is the effort to forget.
Some day I shall be cold, I know,
As is the eternal moonlit snow
Of the high Alps, to which I go—
But ah not yet, not yet!

Vain is the agony of grief.
'Tis true, indeed, an iron knot
Ties straitly up from mine thy lot,
And were it snapt—thou lov'st me not!
10   But is despair relief?

Awhile let me with thought have done.
And as this brimm'd unwrinkled Rhine,
And that far purple mountain-line,
Lie sweetly in the look divine
Of the slow-sinking sun;

So let me lie, and, calm as they,
Let beam upon my inward view
Those eyes of deep, soft, lucent hue—
Eyes too expressive to be blue,
20   Too lovely to be grey.

Ah, Quiet, all things feel thy balm!
Those blue hills too, this river's flow,
Were restless once, but long ago.
Tamed is their turbulent youthful glow;
Their joy is in their calm.

GEORGE MEREDITH (1828–1909)

Lucifer in Starlight

On a starred night Prince Lucifer uprose.
Tired of his dark dominion swung the fiend
Above the rolling ball in cloud part screened,
Where sinners hugged their spectre of repose.
Poor prey to his hot fit of pride were those.
And now upon his western wing he leaned,
Now his huge bulk o'er Afric's sands careened,
Now the black planet shadowed Arctic snows.
Soaring through wider zones that pricked his scars
10 With memory of the old revolt from Awe,
He reached a middle height, and at the stars,
Which are the brain of heaven, he looked, and sank.
Around the ancient track marched, rank on rank,
The army of unalterable law.

DANTE GABRIEL ROSSETTI (1828–1882)

The Woodspurge

The wind flapped loose, the wind was still,
Shaken out dead from tree and hill:
I had walked on at the wind's will,—
I sat now, for the wind was still.

Between my knees my forehead was,—
My lips, drawn in, said not Alas!
My hair was over in the grass,
My naked ears heard the day pass.

My eyes, wide open, had the run
10   Of some ten weeds to fix upon;
Among those few, out of the sun,
The woodspurge flowered, three cups in one.

From perfect grief there need not be
Wisdom or even memory:
One thing then learnt remains to me,—
That woodspurge has a cup of three.

ALBERT BRODRICK (1830–1908)

The Wheel of Fortune

> *There's many a slip*
> *Twixt the 'suff' and the scrip*
> Johannesburg Proverb

Round goes life's wheel, with constant spin—
    Some fellows up, and others under;
And those who lose, and those who win,
    And those who're right, and those who blunder,
Succeed each other, day by day,
Till all, in time, are whirled away!

Here, 'neath these pleasant Afric skies,
    Some men get mended, though thrice 'broken';
And big men sink, and small men rise,
    And scarce a word of wonder spoken!
One moment—with a 'balance' great—
The next they're begging of a mate.

There's Jack, who, in the early days,
    'Voorlooped' for some old Afrikander;
Now (though he spells in artful ways),
    Signs cheques like any rich Uitlander.
And Sam, whose name still runs a Mine,
Is quite uncertain where to dine.

We don't want much, we want *enough*;
    We don't want after coin to grovel:
We want the pleasant 'quantum suff'—
    That keeps us from the pick and shovel.
Let's have enough, and well employ it—
And let some others, too, enjoy it.

There are some men with so much gold—
    They're quite afraid to have much pleasure;
Like some old Boers, who, I've been told—
    Sit with a gun to guard their treasure;
They've got so much they half detest it,
    And howl, because they can't invest it!

Oh! what a life? and what is pelf?
    And what's the good of always hoarding,
When very soon, just for yourself,
    You'll only want some feet of 'boarding'?
You go—and your last will won't mend it;
They'll quarrel o'er your gold, and spend it!

Round goes life's wheel with ceaseless spin,
    Some fellows up, and others under;
And those who lose, and those who win,
40   And those who're right, and those who blunder—
Succeed each other, day by day,
Till all, in time, are swept away!

(p. 248)

Epitaph on a Diamond Digger

Here lies a digger, all his chips departed—
A splint of nature, bright, and ne'er down-hearted:
He worked in many claims, but now (though stumped)
He's got a claim above that can't be jumped.
May he turn out a pure and spotless 'wight',
When the Great Judge shall sift the wrong from right,
And may his soul, released from this low Babel,
Be found a gem on God's great sorting table.

(p. 248)

EMILY DICKINSON (1830–1886)

There came a wind like a bugle

There came a wind like a bugle;
It quivered through the grass,
And a green chill upon the heat
So ominous did pass
We barred the windows and the doors
As from an emerald ghost;
The doom's electric moccasin
That very instant passed.
On a strange mob of panting trees,
And fences fled away,
And rivers where the houses ran
The living looked that day.
The bell within the steeple wild
The flying tidings whirled.
How much can come
And much can go,
And yet abide the world!

10

(p. 248)

They shut me up in prose

They shut me up in prose—
As when a little girl
They put me in the closet—
Because they liked me 'still'—

Still! Could themself have peeped—
And seen my brain—go round—
They might as wise have lodged a bird
For treason—in the pound—

Himself has but to will
And easy as a star
Look down upon captivity—
And laugh—No more have I—

0

There's been a death, in the opposite house

There's been a death, in the opposite house,
As lately as today—
I know it, by the numb look
Such houses have—alway—

The neighbours rustle in and out—
The doctor—drives away—
A window opens like a pod—
Abrupt—mechanically—

Somebody flings a mattress out—
The children hurry by—
They wonder if it died—on that—
I used to—when a boy—

The minister—goes stiffly in—
As if the house were his—
And he owned all the mourners—now—
And little boys—besides—

And then the milliner—and the man
Of the appalling trade—
To take the measure of the house—
There'll be that dark parade—

Of tassles—and of coaches—soon—
It's easy as a sign—
The intuition of the news—
In just a country town—

THOMAS HARDY (1840—1928)

The Voice

Woman much missed, how you call to me, call to me,
Saying that now you are not as you were
When you had changed from the one who was all to me,
But as at first, when our day was fair.

Can it be you that I hear? Let me view you, then,
Standing as when I drew near to the town
Where you would wait for me: yes, as I knew you then,
Even to the original air-blue gown!

Or is it only the breeze, in its listlessness
10   Travelling across the wet mead to me here,
You being ever dissolved to wan wistlessness,
Heard no more again far or near?

       Thus I; faltering forward,
       Leaves around me falling,
Wind oozing thin through the thorn from norward,
       And the woman calling.

During Wind and Rain

      They sing their dearest songs—
      He, she, all of them—yea,
      Treble and tenor and bass,
        And one to play;
      With the candles mooning each face . . .
        Ah, no; the years O!
How the sick leaves reel down in throngs!

      They clear the creeping moss—
      Elders and juniors—aye,
      Making the pathways neat
        And the garden gay;
      And they build a shady seat . . .
        Ah, no; the years, the years;
See, the white storm-birds wing across!

They are blithely breakfasting all—
　　Men and maidens—yea,
　　Under the summer tree,
　　　　With a glimpse of the bay,
　　While pet fowl come to the knee . . .
20　　　　Ah, no; the years O!
And the rotten rose is ript from the wall.

They change to a high new house,
　　He, she, all of them—aye,
　　Clocks and carpets and chairs
　　　　On the lawn all day,
　　And brightest things that are theirs . . .
　　　　Ah, no: the years, the years;
Down their carved names the rain-drop ploughs.

Drummer Hodge

1

They throw in Drummer Hodge, to rest
　　　　Uncoffined—just as found:
His landmark is a kopje-crest
　　　　That breaks the veldt around;
And foreign constellations west
　　　　Each night above his mound.

2

Young Hodge the Drummer never knew—
　　　　Fresh from his Wessex home—
The meaning of the broad Karoo,
10　　　　The Bush, the dusty loam,
And why uprose to nightly view
　　　　Strange stars amid the gloam.

3

Yet portion of that unknown plain
　　　　Will Hodge for ever be;
His homely Northern breast and brain
　　　　Grow to some Southern tree,
And strange-eyed constellations reign
　　　　His stars eternally.

GERARD MANLEY HOPKINS (1844—1889)

Spring and Fall
(to a young child)

Márgarét, áre you gríeving
Over Goldengrove unleaving?
Leáves líke the things of man, you
With your fresh thoughts care for, can you?
Ah! ás the heart grows older
It will come to such sights colder
By and by, nor spare a sigh
Though worlds of wanwood leafmeal lie;
And yet you *will* weep and know why.
10   Now no matter, child, the name:
Sórrow's springs áre the same.
Nor mouth had, no nor mind, expressed
What heart heard of, ghost guessed:
It ís the blight man was born for,
It is Margaret you mourn for.

Hurrahing in Harvest

Summer ends now; now, barbarous in beauty, the stooks rise
    Around; up above, what wind-walks! what lovely behaviour
    Of silk-sack clouds! has wilder, wilful-wavier
Meal-drift moulded ever and melted across skies?

I walk, I lift up, I lift up heart, eyes,
    Down all that glory in the heavens to glean our Saviour;
    And, éyes, heárt, what looks, what lips yet gave you a
Rapturous love's greeting of realer, of rounder replies?

And the azurous hung hills are his world-wielding shoulder
10   Majestic—as a stallion stalwart, very-violet-sweet!—
These things, these things were here and but the beholder
    Wanting; which two when they once meet,
The heart réars wíngs bold and bolder
    And hurls for him, O half curls earth for him off under his feet.

Carrion Comfort

Not, I'll not, carrion comfort, Despair, not feast on thee;
Not untwist—slack they may be—these last strands of man
In me ór, most weary, cry *I can no more.* I can;
Can something, hope, wish day come, not choose not to be.
But ah, but O thou terrible, why wouldst thou rude on me
Thy wring-world right foot rock? lay a lionlimb against me? scan
With darksome devouring eyes my bruisèd bones? and fan,
O in turns of tempest, me heaped there; me frantic to avoid thee
    and flee?

Why? That my chaff might fly; my grain lie, sheer and clear.
10   Nay in all that toil, that coil, since (seems) I kissed the rod,
Hand rather, my heart lo! lapped strength, stole joy, would laugh,
    chéer.
Cheer whom though? the hero whose heaven-handling flung me,
    fóot tród
Me? or me that fought him? O which one? is it each one? That
    night, that year
Of now done darkness I wretch lay wrestling with (my God!) my
    God.

RUDYARD KIPLING (1865–1936)

Stellenbosh

The General 'eard the firin' on the flank,
    An' 'e sent a mounted man to bring 'im back
The silly, pushin' person's name an' rank
    'Oo'd dared to answer Brother Boer's attack.
For there might 'ave been a serious engagement,
    An' 'e might 'ave wasted 'alf a dozen men;
So 'e ordered 'im to stop 'is operations round the kopjes,
    An' 'e told 'im off before the Staff at ten!

        And it all goes into the laundry,
10   But it never comes out in the wash,
        'Ow we're sugared about by the old men
        ('Eavy-sterned amateur old men!)
        That 'amper an' 'inder an' scold men
        For fear o' Stellenbosh!

The General 'ad 'produced a great effect',
    The General 'ad the country cleared—almost;
The General ''ad no reason to expect',
    And the Boers 'ad us bloomin' well on toast!
For we might 'ave crossed the drift before the twilight,
20   Instead o' sitting down an' takin' root;
But we was not allowed, so the Boojers scooped the crowd,
    To the last survivin' bandolier an' boot.

The General saw the farm'ouse in 'is rear,
    With its stoep so nicely shaded from the sun;
Sez 'e, 'I'll pitch my tabernacle 'ere,'
    An' 'e kept us muckin' round till 'e 'ad done.
For 'e might 'ave caught the confluent pneumonia
    From sleepin' in his gaiters in the dew;
So 'e took a book an' dozed while the other columns closed,
30   And De Wet's commando out an' trickled through!

The General saw the mountain-range ahead,
    With their 'elios showin' saucy on the 'eight,
So 'e 'eld us to the level ground instead,
    An' telegraphed the Boojers wouldn't fight.
For 'e might 'ave gone an' sprayed 'em with a pompom,
    Or 'e might 'ave slung a squadron out to see—
But 'e wasn't takin' chances in them 'igh an' 'ostile kranzes—
    He was markin' time to earn a K.C.B.

The General got 'is decorations thick
40   (The men that backed 'is lies could not complain),
The Staff 'ad D.S.O.'s till we was sick,
    An' the soldier—'ad the work to do again!
For 'e might 'ave known the District was a 'otbed,
    Instead of 'andin' over, upside-down,
To a man 'oo 'ad to fight 'alf a year to put it right,
    While the General went an' slandered 'im in town!

        An' it all went into the laundry,
        But it never came out in the wash.
        We were sugared about by the old men
50   (Panicky, perishin' old men)
        That 'amper an' 'inder an' scold men
        For fear o' Stellenbosh!

(p. 248)

M. GROVER (dates unknown)

I killed a man at Graspan
(The Tale of a Returned Australian Contingenter done into verse)

I killed a man at Graspan,
   I killed him fair in a fight;
And the Empire's poets and the Empire's priests
   Swear blind I acted right.
The Empire's poets and Empire's priests
   Make out my deed was fine,
But they can't stop the eyes of the man I killed
   From starin' into mine.

I killed a man at Graspan,
10   Maybe I killed a score;
But this one wasn't a chance-shot home,
   From a thousand yards or more.
I fired at him when he'd got no show;
   We were only a pace apart,
With the cordite scorchin' his old worn coat
   As the bullet drilled his heart.

I killed a man at Graspan,
   I killed him fightin' fair;
We came on each other face to face,
20   An' we went at it then and there.
Mine was the trigger that shifted first,
   His was the life that sped.
An' a man I'd never a quarrel with
   Was spread on the boulders dead.

I killed a man at Graspan;
   I watched him squirmin' till
He raised his eyes, an' they met with mine;
   An' there they're starin' still.
Cut of my brother Tom, he looked,
30   Hardly more'n a kid;
An', Christ! he was stiffenin' at my feet
   Because of the thing I did.

I killed a man at Graspan;
   I told the camp that night;
An' of all the lies that ever I told
   That was the poorest skite.
I swore I was proud of my hand-to-hand,
   An' the Boer I'd chanced to pot,
An' all the time I'd ha' gave my eyes
40   To never ha' fired that shot.

I killed a man at Graspan;
   An hour ago about;
For there he lies with his starin' eyes,
   An' his blood still tricklin' out.
I know it was either him or me,
   I know that I killed him fair,
But, all the same, wherever I look,
   The man that I killed is there.

I killed a man at Graspan;
50   My first and, God! my last;
Harder to dodge than my bullet is
   The look that his dead eyes cast.
If the Empire asks for me later on
   It'll ask for me in vain,
Before I reach to my bandolier
   To fire on a man again.

(p. 249)

128

W.B. YEATS (1865–1939)

No Second Troy

Why should I blame her that she filled my days
With misery, or that she would of late
Have taught to ignorant men most violent ways,
Or hurled the little streets upon the great,
Had they but courage equal to desire?
What could have made her peaceful with a mind
That nobleness made simple as a fire,
With beauty like a tightened bow, a kind
That is not natural in an age like this,
10   Being high and solitary and most stern?
Why, what could she have done, being what she is?
Was there another Troy for her to burn?

(p. 249)

Easter 1916

I have met them at close of day
Coming with vivid faces
From counter or desk among grey
Eighteenth-century houses.
I have passed with a nod of the head
Or polite meaningless words,
Or have lingered awhile and said
Polite meaningless words,
And thought before I had done
10   Of a mocking tale or a gibe
To please a companion
Around the fire at the club,
Being certain that they and I
But lived where motley is worn:
All changed, changed utterly:
A terrible beauty is born.

That woman's days were spent
In ignorant good-will,
Her nights in argument
20   Until her voice grew shrill.
What voice more sweet than hers
When, young and beautiful,
She rode to harriers?
This man had kept a school
And rode our wingèd horse;
This other his helper and friend
Was coming into his force;
He might have won fame in the end,
So sensitive his nature seemed,
30   So daring and sweet his thought.
This other man I had dreamed
A drunken, vainglorious lout.
He had done most bitter wrong
To some who are near my heart,
Yet I number him in the song;
He, too, has resigned his part
In the casual comedy;
He, too, has been changed in his turn,
Transformed utterly:
40   A terrible beauty is born.

Hearts with one purpose alone
Through summer and winter seem
Enchanted to a stone
To trouble the living stream.
The horse that comes from the road,
The rider, the birds that range
From cloud to tumbling cloud,
Minute by minute they change;
A shadow of cloud on the stream
50   Changes minute by minute;
A horse-hoof slides on the brim,
And a horse plashes within it;
The long-legged moor-hens dive,
And hens to moor-cocks call;
Minute by minute they live:
The stone's in the midst of all.

Too long a sacrifice
Can make a stone of the heart.
O when may it suffice?
60 That is Heaven's part, our part
To murmur name upon name,
As a mother names her child
When sleep at last has come
On limbs that had run wild.
What is it but nightfall?
No, no, not night but death;
Was it needless death after all?
For England may keep faith
For all that is done and said.
70 We know their dream; enough
To know they dreamed and are dead;
And what if excess of love
Bewildered them till they died?
I write it out in a verse—
MacDonagh and MacBride
And Connolly and Pearse
Now and in time to be,
Wherever green is worn,
Are changed, changed utterly:
80 A terrible beauty is born.

September 25, 1916

(p. 249)

On a Political Prisoner

She that but little patience knew,
From childhood on, had now so much
A grey gull lost its fear and flew
Down to her cell and there alit,
And there endured her fingers' touch
And from her fingers ate its bit.

Did she in touching that lone wing
Recall the years before her mind
Became a bitter, an abstract thing,

10   Her thought some popular enmity:
        Blind and leader of the blind
        Drinking the foul ditch where they lie?

        When long ago I saw her ride
        Under Ben Bulben to the meet,
        The beauty of her country-side
        With all youth's lonely wildness stirred,
        She seemed to have grown clean and sweet
        Like any rock-bred, sea-borne bird:

        Sea-borne, or balanced on the air
20   When first it sprang out of the nest
        Upon some lofty rock to stare
        Upon the cloudy canopy,
        While under its storm-beaten breast
        Cried out the hollows of the sea.

(p. 249)

The Man and the Echo

Man

        In a cleft that's christened Alt
        Under broken stone I halt
        At the bottom of a pit
        That broad noon has never lit,
        And shout a secret to the stone.
        All that I have said and done,
        Now that I am old and ill,
        Turns into a question till
        I lie awake night after night
10   And never get the answers right.
        Did that play of mine send out
        Certain men the English shot?
        Did words of mine put too great strain
        On that woman's reeling brain?
        Could my spoken words have checked
        That whereby a house lay wrecked?
        And all seems evil until I
        Sleepless would lie down and die.

Lie down and die.

20   That were to shirk
The spiritual intellect's great work,
And shirk it in vain. There is no release
In a bodkin or disease,
Nor can there be work so great
As that which cleans man's dirty slate.
While man can still his body keep
Wine or love drug him to sleep,
Waking he thanks the Lord that he
Has body and its stupidity,
30 But body gone he sleeps no more,
And till his intellect grows sure
That all's arranged in one clear view,
Pursues the thoughts that I pursue,
Then stands in judgement on his soul,
And, all work done, dismisses all
Out of intellect and sight
And sinks at last into the night.

Into the night.

    O Rocky Voice,
40 Shall we in that great night rejoice?
What do we know but that we face
One another in this place?
But hush, for I have lost the theme,
Its joy or night seem but a dream;
Up there some hawk or owl has struck,
Dropping out of sky or rock,
A stricken rabbit is crying out,
And its cry distracts my thought.

CHARLES CLAYBROOK WOLLACOTT (1873–?)

The Abandoned Mine

A heap of rock marks the abandoned mine.
   The veld's unpitying silence lies around
Those broken stones—a mute and mournful sign
   Of human enterprise with failure crowned.
Here is the trail along which used to pass
   The workers to and fro: a narrow track
That winds away among the bush and grass—
   But those who trod it will no more come back!

Time, with slow hands, shall from the scene anew
10   Repair the gashes in the wounded soil,
And cover up the last remaining clue
   To a poor useless record of men's toil.
And this, the mound they built when hopes were high,
Shall be a grave, where those hopes buried lie.

ROBERT FROST (1875–1963)

Stopping by Woods on a Snowy Evening

Whose woods these are I think I know.
His house is in the village though;
He will not see me stopping here
To watch his woods fill up with snow.

My little horse must think it queer
To stop without a farmhouse near
Between the woods and frozen lake
The darkest evening of the year.

He gives his harness bells a shake
To ask if there is some mistake.
The only other sound's the sweep
Of easy wind and downy flake.

The woods are lovely, dark and deep,
But I have promises to keep,
And miles to go before I sleep,
And miles to go before I sleep.

Design

I found a dimpled spider, fat and white,
On a white heal-all, holding up a moth
Like a white piece of rigid satin cloth—
Assorted characters of death and blight
Mixed ready to begin the morning right,
Like the ingredients of a witch's broth—
A snow-drop spider, a flower like froth,
And dead wings carried like a paper kite.

What had that flower to do with being white,
The wayside blue and innocent heal-all?
What brought the kindred spider to that height,
Then steered the white moth thither in the night?
What but design of darkness to appall?—
If design govern in a thing so small.

(p. 249)

35

FRANCIS CAREY SLATER (1876–1958)

Xhosa Road-Menders' Chant

Hard are the stones on this highway,
Rough as the hide of a crocodile,
Hard, but our hammers shall break them,
Rough, but our manhood shall make them
Smooth as the wings of a wild-dove,
Sleek as the hide of a heifer.
Yes, we shall break them and make them
Smooth for the wheels of the white man,
Soft for the barefooted black man.

10   *Zamani, zamani! Siyavuma!*

Rough are the laws of our rulers,
Harsh as the quills of a porcupine,
Hard as the stones on the highway—
Hard, but in patience we labour,
With pick-axes moving high mountains,
With hammers crushing hard boulders:
Steadfast and hopeful we struggle,
Knowing time's tools shall not falter
In moving high mountains of hatred

20   Breaking bonds more stubborn than boulders.
      Zamani, zamani! Siyavuma!

10 Struggle on, struggle on! We agree!

(p. 249)

Xhosa Proverb

'The ox is skinned on one side only.'
    Ponder well this saw, and do not go to law,
    For, like ox with half-a-hide, justice has oft one side.

WALLACE STEVENS (1879–1955)

The Poems of Our Climate

1

Clear water in a brilliant bowl,
Pink and white carnations. The light
In the room more like a snowy air,
Reflecting snow. A newly-fallen snow
At the end of winter when afternoons return.
Pink and white carnations—one desires
So much more than that. The day itself
Is simplified: a bowl of white,
Cold, a cold porcelain, low and round,
With nothing more than the carnations there.

2

Say even that this complete simplicity
Stripped one of all one's torments, concealed
The evilly compounded, vital I
And made it fresh in a world of white,
A world of clear water, brilliant-edged,
Still one would want more, one would need more,
More than a world of white and snowy scents.

3

There would still remain the never-resting mind,
So that one would want to escape, come back
To what had been so long composed.
The imperfect is our paradise.
Note that, in this bitterness, delight,
Since the imperfect is so hot in us,
Lies in flawed words and stubborn sounds.

WILLIAM CARLOS WILLIAMS (1883–1963)

The Red Wheelbarrow

so much depends
upon

a red wheel
barrow

glazed with rain
water

beside the white
chickens.

The Lonely Street

School is over. It is too hot
to walk at ease. At ease
in light frocks they walk the streets
to while the time away.
They have grown tall. They hold
pink flames in their right hands.
In white from head to foot,
with sidelong, idle look—
in yellow, floating stuff,
black sash and stockings—
touching their avid mouths
with pink sugar on a stick—
like a carnation each holds in her hand—
they mount the lonely street.

KINGSLEY FAIRBRIDGE (1885–1924)

Bongwi

A haunted soul put under ban,
    A hunted beast that has to roam,
The voiceless image of a man
    With neither speech nor home—
Upon the summit of the height,
    Where only wind-swept lichens grow,
Bongwi, lit by the dawning-light,
    Watches the plain below.

Fierce eyes, low brow, protruding mouth,
10   Short hands that twitch and twitch again,
The hairy gargoyle of the South—
    A man without a brain;
Upon the highest krantz he waits
    Dim-lit by golden streak of dawn,
Guarding the interests of his mates
    Who wreck the fields of corn.

Far down the mealie-gardens lie,
    And he, a patient sentinel,
Shouts 'Boor-hoom!' to th' offended sky
20   To show that all is well.
A white fish-eagle sails along,
    His mighty pinions harping tunes,
Till dawn throbs with Aeolian song
    And, far below, the brown baboons

Look up and note the paling East,
    The fading moon, the stars that wane,
And, gorg'd, they quit their stolen feast
    And seek the open veld again.
And Bongwi sees. But turns his view—
30   Brown-eyed—towards the breaking morn,
And gazes through the soundless blue,
    The golden distance of the dawn.

D.H. LAWRENCE (1885–1930)

Afternoon in School
The Last Lesson

When will the bell ring, and end this weariness?
How long have they tugged the leash, and strained apart
My pack of unruly hounds: I cannot start
Them again on a quarry of knowledge they hate to hunt,
I can haul them and urge them no more.
No more can I endure to bear the brunt
Of the books that lie out on the desks: a full three score
Of several insults of blotted pages and scrawl
Of slovenly work that they have offered me.
10   I am sick, and tired more than any thrall
Upon the woodstacks working weariedly.

                            And shall I take
The last dear fuel and heap it on my soul
Till I rouse my will like a fire to consume
Their dross of indifference, and burn the scroll
Of their insults in punishment?—I will not!
I will not waste myself to embers for them,
Not all for them shall the fires of my life be hot,
For myself a heap of ashes of weariness, till sleep
Shall have raked the embers clear: I will keep
20   Some of my strength for myself, for if I should sell
It all for them, I should hate them—
                    —I will sit and wait for the bell.

Giorno Dei Morti

Along the avenue of cypresses
All in their scarlet cloaks, and surplices
Of linen go the chanting choristers,
The priests in gold and black, the villagers . . .

And all along the path to the cemetery
The round dark heads of men crowd silently,
And black-scarved faces of women-folk, wistfully
Watch at the banner of death, and the mystery.

And at the foot of a grave a father stands
10   With sunken head, and forgotten, folded hands;
And at the foot of a grave a mother kneels
With pale shut face, nor either hears nor feels

The coming of the chanting choristers
Between the avenue of cypresses,
The silence of the many villagers,
The candle-flames beside the surplices.

(title): Day of the Dead

Whatever Man Makes

Whatever man makes and makes it live
lives because of the life put into it.
A yard of India muslin is alive with Hindu life.
And a Navajo woman, weaving her rug in the pattern of her dream
must run the pattern out in a little break at the end
so that her soul can come out, back to her.

But in the odd pattern, like snake-marks on the sand
it leaves its trail.

EZRA POUND (1885–1972)

In a Station of the Metro

The apparition of these faces in the crowd;
Petals on a wet, black bough.

The River-Merchant's Wife: A Letter

While my hair was still cut straight across my forehead
I played about the front gate, pulling flowers.
You came by on bamboo stilts, playing horse,
You walked about my seat, playing with blue plums.
And we went on living in the village of Chokan:
Two small people, without dislike or suspicion.

At fourteen I married My Lord you.
I never laughed, being bashful.
Lowering my head, I looked at the wall.
10 Called to, a thousand times, I never looked back.

At fifteen I stopped scowling,
I desired my dust to be mingled with yours
For ever and for ever and for ever.
Why should I climb the look out?

At sixteen you departed,
You went into far Ku-to-yen, by the river of swirling eddies,
And you have been gone five months.
The monkeys make sorrowful noise overhead.

You dragged your feet when you went out.
20 By the gate now, the moss is grown, the different mosses,
Too deep to clear them away!
The leaves fall early this autumn, in wind.
The paired butterflies are already yellow with August
Over the grass in the West garden;
They hurt me, I grow older.
If you are coming down through the narrows of the river Kiang,
Please let me know beforehand,
And I will come out to meet you
                    As far as Cho-fu-Sa.

(By Rihaku)

T.S. ELIOT (1888–1965)

Rhapsody on a Windy Night

Twelve o'clock.
Along the reaches of the street
Held in a lunar synthesis,
Whispering lunar incantations
Dissolve the floors of memory
And all its clear relations,
Its divisions and precisions,
Every street lamp that I pass
Beats like a fatalistic drum,
And through the spaces of the dark
Midnight shakes the memory
As a madman shakes a dead geranium.

    Half-past one,
The street-lamp sputtered,
The street-lamp muttered,
The street-lamp said, 'Regard that woman
Who hesitates toward you in the light of the door
Which opens on her like a grin.
You see the border of her dress
Is torn and stained with sand,
And you see the corner of her eye
Twists like a crooked pin.'

    The memory throws up high and dry
A crowd of twisted things;
A twisted branch upon the beach
Eaten smooth, and polished
As if the world gave up
The secret of its skeleton,
Stiff and white.
A broken spring in a factory yard,
Rust that clings to the form that the strength has left
Hard and curled and ready to snap.

Half-past two,
The street-lamp said,
'Remark the cat which flattens itself in the gutter,
Slips out its tongue
And devours a morsel of rancid butter.'
So the hand of the child, automatic,
Slipped out and pocketed a toy that was running along the quay.
40 I could see nothing behind that child's eye.
I have seen eyes in the street
Trying to peer through lighted shutters,
And a crab one afternoon in a pool,
An old crab with barnacles on his back,
Gripped the end of a stick which I held him.

    Half-past three,
The lamp sputtered,
The lamp muttered in the dark.
The lamp hummed:
50 'Regard the moon,
La lune ne garde aucune rancune,
She winks a feeble eye,
She smiles into corners.
She smooths the hair of the grass.
The moon has lost her memory.

    'A washed-out smallpox cracks her face,
Her hand twists a paper rose,
That smells of dust and eau de Cologne,
She is alone
60 With all the old nocturnal smells
That cross and cross across her brain.'
The reminiscence comes
Of sunless dry geraniums
And dust in crevices,
Smells of chestnuts in the streets,
And female smells in shuttered rooms
And cigarettes in corridors
And cocktail smells in bars.

51 The moon does not bear any grudge.

The lamp said,
70 'Four o'clock,
Here is the number on the door.
Memory!
You have the key,
The little lamp spreads a ring on the stair.
Mount.
The bed is open; the tooth-brush hangs on the wall,
Put your shoes at the door, sleep, prepare for life.'

The last twist of the knife.

JOHN CROWE RANSOM (1888–1974)

Bells for John Whiteside's Daughter

There was such speed in her little body,
And such lightness in her footfall,
It is no wonder her brown study
Astonishes us all.

Her wars were bruited in our high window.
We looked among orchard trees and beyond
Where she took arms against her shadow,
Or harried unto the pond

10   The lazy geese, like a snow cloud
Dripping their snow on the green grass,
Tricking and stopping, sleepy and proud,
Who cried in goose, Alas,

For the tireless heart within the little
Lady with rod that made them rise
From their noon apple-dreams and scuttle
Goose-fashion under the skies!

But now go the bells, and we are ready,
In one house we are sternly stopped
To say we are vexed at her brown study,
20   Lying so primly propped.

WILFRED OWEN (1893–1918)

Dulce et Decorum Est

Bent double, like old beggars under sacks,
Knock-kneed, coughing like hags, we cursed through sludge,
Till on the haunting flares we turned our backs
And towards our distant rest began to trudge.
Men marched asleep. Many had lost their boots
But limped on, blood-shod. All went lame; all blind;
Drunk with fatigue; deaf even to the hoots
Of tired, outstripped Five-Nines that dropped behind.

Gas! Gas! Quick, boys!—An ecstasy of fumbling,
10   Fitting the clumsy helmets just in time;
But someone still was yelling out and stumbling
And flound'ring like a man in fire or lime . . .
Dim, through the misty panes and thick green light,
As under a green sea, I saw him drowning.

In all my dreams, before my helpless sight,
He plunges at me, guttering, choking, drowning.

If in some smothering dreams you too could pace
Behind the wagon that we flung him in,
And watch the white eyes writhing in his face,
20   His hanging face, like a devil's sick of sin;
If you could hear, at every jolt, the blood
Come gargling from the froth-corrupted lungs,
Obscene as cancer, bitter as the cud
Of vile, incurable sores on innocent tongues,—
My friend, you would not tell with such high zest
To children ardent for some desperate glory,
The old Lie: *Dulce et decorum est
Pro patria mori.*

27–28 'It is sweet and fitting to die for one's country.' (Horace, the Roman poet)
(p. 249)

e.e. cummings (1894–1963)

my sweet old etcetera

my sweet old etcetera
aunt lucy during the recent

war could and what
is more did tell you just
what everybody was fighting .

for,
my sister

isabel created hundreds
(and
10   hundreds) of socks not to
mention shirts fleaproof earwarmers

etcetera wristers etcetera, my
mother hoped that

i would die etcetera
bravely of course my father used
to become hoarse talking about how it was
a privilege and if only he
could meanwhile my

self etcetera lay quietly
20   in the deep mud et

cetera
(dreaming,
et
    cetera, of
Your smile
eyes knees and of your Etcetera)

(p. 249)

ygUDuh

          ydoan
          yunnuhstan

          ydoan o
          yunnuhstan dem
          yguduh ged

          yunnuhstan dem doidee
          yguduh ged riduh
          ydoan o nudn
LISN bud LISN

10   dem
                     gud
                     am

                     lidl yelluh bas
                     tuds weer goin

duhSIVILEYEzum

Buffalo Bill's

Buffalo Bill's
defunct
          who used to
          ride a watersmooth-silver
                                        stallion
and break onetwothreefourfive pigeonsjustlikethat
                                             Jesus

he was a handsome man
                         and what i want to know is
10   how do you like your blueeyed boy
Mister Death

49

ROBERT GRAVES (1895–1985)

The Cool Web

Children are dumb to say how hot the day is,
How hot the scent is of the summer rose,
How dreadful the black wastes of evening sky,
How dreadful the tall soldiers drumming by.

But we have speech, to chill the angry day,
And speech, to dull the rose's cruel scent.
We spell away the overhanging night,
We spell away the soldiers and the fright.

There's a cool web of language winds us in,
10   Retreat from too much joy or too much fear:
We grow sea-green at last and coldly die
In brininess and volubility.

But if we let our tongues lose self-possession,
Throwing off language and its watery clasp
Before our death, instead of when death comes,
Facing the wide glare of the children's day,
Facing the rose, the dark sky and the drums
We shall go mad no doubt and die that way.

Counting the Beats

You, love, and I,
(He whispers) you and I,
And if no more than only you and I
What care you or I?

Counting the beats,
Counting the slow heart beats,
The bleeding to death of time in slow heart beats,
Wakeful they lie.

Cloudless day,
10   Night, and a cloudless day,
Yet the huge storm will burst upon their heads one day
From a bitter sky.

Where shall we be,
(She whispers) where shall we be,
When death strikes home, O where then shall we be
Who were you and I?

Not there but here,
(He whispers) only here,
As we are, here, together, now and here,
20   Always you and I.

Counting the beats,
Counting the slow heart beats,
The bleeding to death of time in slow heart beats,
Wakeful they lie.

CHARLES OULD (1898–1971)

Voortrekkers

Over the silent horizons,
In the unknown,
There was a country that called them,
Lovely and lone.

Distant, unknown lay the country,
Danger between;
They took their wagons and oxen
And sought the unseen.

Farther they travelled and farther;
10 Paused from their quest.
Still came a voice from the distance:
'Not there is rest.'

They are dead and all countries discovered.
Now but in thought
Beckons that fugitive beauty,
Still to be sought.

A country of peace and attainment
Smiles to the sun,
Beckoning, beckoning,
20 Not to be won.

ST J. PAGE YAKO (1900–1971)

The Contraction and Enclosure of the Land

Thus spake the heirs of the land
Although it is no longer ours.
This land will be folded like a blanket
Till it is like the palm of a hand.
The racing ox will become entangled in the wire,
Too weak to dance free, it will be worn
Out by the dance of the yoke and the plough.
They will crowd us together like tadpoles
In a calabash ladle. Our girls
10 Will have their lobola paid with paper,
Coins that come and go, come and go.
Blood should not be spilled, so they say
Nowadays, to unite the different peoples;
Until we no longer care for each other,
As a cow licks her calf, when love
And nature urges her to do so.
Can money bring people together?
Yes, a man may have words with his son's wife,
His son need no longer respect her mother.

20 Yes, we fold up our knees,
It's impossible to stretch out,
Because the land has been hedged in.

(trans. from the Xhosa)

ROY CAMPBELL (1901–1957)

The Theology of Bongwi, the Baboon

This is the wisdom of the Ape
    Who yelps beneath the Moon—
'Tis God who made me in His shape
    He is a Great Baboon.
'Tis He who tilts the moon askew
    And fans the forest trees,
The heavens which are broad and blue
    Provide him his trapeze;
He swings with tail divinely bent
10   Around those azure bars
And munches to his Soul's content
    The kernels of the stars;
And when I die, His loving care
    Will raise me from the sod
To learn the perfect Mischief there,
    The Nimbleness of God.

The Serf

His naked skin clothed in the torrid mist
That puffs in smoke around the patient hooves,
The ploughman drives, a slow somnambulist,
And through the green his crimson furrow grooves.
His heart, more deeply than he wounds the plain,
Long by the rasping share of insult torn,
Red clod, to which the war-cry once was rain
And tribal spears the fatal sheaves of corn,
Lies fallow now. But as the turf divides
10 I see in the slow progress of his strides
Over the toppled clods and falling flowers,
The timeless, surly patience of the serf
That moves the nearest to the naked earth
And ploughs down palaces, and thrones, and towers.

Autumn

I love to see, when leaves depart,
The clear anatomy arrive,
Winter, the paragon of art,
That kills all forms of life and feeling
Save what is pure and will survive.

Already now the clanging chains
Of geese are harnessed to the moon:
Stripped are the great sun-clouding planes:
And the dark pines, their own revealing,
Let in the needles of the noon.

Strained by the gale the olives whiten
Like hoary wrestlers bent with toil
And, with the vines, their branches lighten
To brim our vats where summer lingers
In the red froth and sun-gold oil.

Soon on our hearth's reviving pyre
Their rotted stems will crumble up:
And like a ruby, panting fire,
The grape will redden on your fingers
Through the lit crystal of the cup.

Epigrams

Holism

The love of Nature burning in his heart,
Our new Saint Francis offers us his book—
The saint who fed the birds at Bondleswaart
And fattened up the vultures at Bull Hoek.

On Some South African Novelists

You praise the firm restraint with which they write—
I'm with you there, of course:
They use the snaffle and the curb all right,
But where's the bloody horse?

. 249)

J.J.R. JOLOBE (1902—1976)

The Making of a Servant

I can no longer ask how it feels
To be choked by a yoke-rope
Because I have seen it for myself in the chained ox.
The blindness has left my eyes. I have become aware,
I have seen the making of a servant
In the young yoke-ox.

He was sleek, lovely, born for freedom,
Not asking anything from any one, simply
      priding himself on being a young ox.
10 Someone said: Let him be caught and
      trained and broken in,
Going about it as if he meant to help him.
I have seen the making of a servant
In the young yoke-ox.

He tried to resist, fighting for his freedom.
He was surrounded, fenced in with wisdom and experience.
They overcame him by trickery: 'He must be trained.'
A good piece of rationalisation can camouflage evil.
I have seen the making of a servant
20 *In the young yoke-ox.*

He was bound with ropes that cut into his head,
He was bullied, kicked, now and again petted,
But their aim was the same: to put a yoke on him.
Being trained in one's own interests is for the privileged.
I have seen the making of a servant
In the young yoke-ox.

The last stage. The yoke is set on him.
They tie the halter round his neck, slightly choking him.
They say the job's done, he'll be put out to work with the others
30 To obey the will of his owner and taskmaster.
I have seen the making of a servant
In the young yoke-ox.

He kicks out, trying to break away.
They speak with their whips. He turns backwards
Doing his best to resist but then they say: 'Hit him.'
A prisoner is a coward's plaything.
I have seen the making of a servant
In the young yoke-ox.

Though he stumbled and fell, he was bitten on the tail.
Sometimes I saw him raking at his yoke-mate
With his horns—his friend of a minute, his blood-brother.
The suffering under the yoke makes for bad blood.
I have seen the making of a servant
In the young yoke-ox.

The sky seemed black as soft rain fell.
I looked at his hump, it was red,
Dripping blood, the mark of resistance.
He yearns for his home, where he was free.
I have seen the making of a servant
In the young yoke-ox.

Stockstill, tired, there was no sympathy.
He bellowed notes of bitterness.
They loosened his halter a little—to let him breathe,
They tightened it again, snatching back his breath.
I have seen the making of a servant
In the young yoke-ox.

I saw him later, broken, trained,
Pulling a double-shared plough through deep soil,
Serving, struggling for breath, in pain.
To be driven is death. Life is doing things for yourself.
I have seen the making of a servant
In the young yoke-ox.

I saw him climb the steepest of roads.
He carried heavy loads, staggering—
The mud of sweat which wins profit for another.
The savour of working is a share in the harvest.
I have seen the making of a servant
In the young yoke-ox.

I saw him hungry with toil and sweat,
70   Eyes all tears, spirit crushed,
No longer able to resist. He was tame.
Hope lies in action aimed at freedom.
I have seen the making of a servant
In the young yoke-ox.

(trans. from the Xhosa)

WILLIAM PLOMER (1903—1973)

The Scorpion

Limpopo and Tugela churned
In flood for brown and angry miles
Melons, maize, domestic thatch,
The trunks of trees and crocodiles;

The swollen estuaries were thick
With flotsam, in the sun one saw
The corpse of a young negress bruised
By rocks, and rolling on the shore,

Pushed by the waves of morning, rolled
Impersonally among shells,
With lolling breasts and bleeding eyes,
And round her neck were beads and bells.

That was the Africa we knew,
Where, wandering alone,
We saw, heraldic in the heat,
A scorpion on a stone.

The Big-Game Hunter

A big-game hunter opens fire once more,
Raconteur, roué, sportsman, millionaire and bore—
But only shoots his mouth off, knowing how
He's safer on a sofa than on far safari now.

L.R.

'Civilised' Labour Policy

Hertzog is my shepherd; I am in want.
He maketh me to lie down on park benches.
He leadeth me beside still factories.
He arouseth my doubt of his intention.
He leadeth me in the path of destruction for his Party's sake.
Yea, I walk through the valley of the shadow of destruction.
And I fear evil, for thou art with me.
The Politicians and the Profiteers, they frighten me,
Thou preparest a reduction in my salary before me,
10 In the presence of mine enemies.
Thou anointest mine income with taxes,
My expense runneth over.
Surely unemployment and poverty will follow me
All the days of this Administration
And I shall dwell in a mortgaged house forever.

(1932)

(p. 249)

160

LÉOPOLD SÉDAR SENGHOR (1906–   )

All Day Long

All day long along the long straight rails
(Unbending will on the listless sands)
Across the dryness of Cayor and Baol where the arms of the
    baobabs twist in anguish
All day long, all along the line
Through tiny stations, each exactly like the last, chattering little
    black girls uncaged from school
All day long, roughly shaken on the benches of the clanking,
    dust-covered, wheezing, antique train
I come seeking to forget about Europe in the pastoral heart of Sine.

(trans. from the French)

p. 250)

W.H. AUDEN (1907–1973)

The Fall of Rome

The piers are pummeled by the waves;
In a lonely field the rain
Lashes an abandoned train;
Outlaws fill the mountain caves.

Fantastic grow the evening gowns;
Agents of the Fisc pursue
Absconding tax-defaulters through
The sewers of provincial towns.

Private rites of magic send
10 The temple prostitutes to sleep;
All the literati keep
An imaginary friend.

Cerebrotonic Catos may
Extol the Ancient Disciplines,
But the muscle-bound Marines
Mutiny for food and pay.

Caesar's double-bed is warm
As an unimportant clerk
Writes *I do not like my work*
20 On a pink official form.

Unendowed with wealth or pity,
Little birds with scarlet legs,
Sitting on their speckled eggs,
Eye each flu-infected city.

Altogether elsewhere, vast
Herds of reindeer move across
Miles and miles of golden moss,
Silently and very fast.

(p. 250)

Song: As I walked out one evening

As I walked out one evening,
    Walking down Bristol Street,
The crowds upon the pavement
    Were fields of harvest wheat.

And down by the brimming river
    I heard a lover sing
Under an arch of the railway:
    'Love has no ending.

'I'll love you, dear, I'll love you
    Till China and Africa meet
And the river jumps over the moutain
    And the salmon sing in the street.

'I'll love you till the ocean
    Is folded and hung up to dry
And the seven stars go squawking
    Like geese about the sky.

'The years shall run like rabbits
    For in my arms I hold
The Flower of the Ages
    And the first love of the world.'

But all the clocks in the city
    Began to whirr and chime:
'O let not Time deceive you,
    You cannot conquer Time.

'In the burrows of the Nightmare
    Where Justice naked is,
Time watches from the shadow
    And coughs when you would kiss.

'In headaches and in worry
    Vaguely life leaks away,
And Time will have his fancy
    Tomorrow or today.

'Into many a green valley
     Drifts the appalling snow;
Time breaks the threaded dances
     And the diver's brilliant bow.

'O plunge your hands in water,
     Plunge them in up to the wrist;
Stare, stare in the basin
40   And wonder what you've missed.

'The glacier knocks in the cupboard,
     The desert sighs in the bed,
And the crack in the tea-cup opens
     A lane to the land of the dead.

'Where the beggars raffle the banknotes
     And the Giant is enchanting to Jack,
And the Lily-white Boy is a Roarer
     And Jill goes down on her back.

'O look, look in the mirror,
50   O look in your distress;
Life remains a blessing
     Although you cannot bless.

'O stand, stand at the window
     As the tears scald and start;
You shall love your crooked neighbour
     With your crooked heart.'

It was late, late in the evening
     The lovers they were gone;
The clocks had ceased their chiming
60   And the deep river ran on.

VINCENT SWART (1911—1962)

Casey Jones

Casey Jones has left today,
The decision was made in a desperate way,
Short as a wire and quick as a plane
And he isn't going to see any of you again.
There was no kind of good in staying on
When the delight was gone.

His hand at the welding was unsteady for months,
And the boss came very near sacking him once.
No rain for weeks: the old mower in pawn,
10   It was an impossible pastime cutting the lawn.
There was no kind of good in staying on
When the delight was gone.

Cries in the head were making him light,
He found it difficult sleeping at night,
The warmth of the women was a shocking reward,
And their unfortunate wishes were growing weird.
There was no kind of good in staying on
When the delight was gone.

O where did he head for? The wind in the wood,
20   And the goat on the tether was coughing up blood,
The clock on the church was pointing at ten
As he passed by the women and left the men.
There was no kind of good in staying on
When the delight was gone.

O where was he going? He didn't quite know,
For vague as a bandage the infected go,
And the mind must follow the deceived decision
Of the night before and the dream's incision.
There was no kind of good in staying on
30   When the delight was gone.

JOHN BERRYMAN (1914–1972)

The Ball Poem

What is the boy now, who has lost his ball,
What, what is he to do? I saw it go
Merrily bouncing, down the street, and then
Merrily over—there it is in the water!
No use to say 'O there are other balls':
An ultimate shaking grief fixes the boy
As he stands rigid, trembling, staring down
All his young days into the harbour where
His ball went. I would not intrude on him,
10   A dime, another ball, is worthless. Now
He senses first responsibility
In a world of possessions. People will take balls,
Balls will be lost always, little boy,
And no one buys a ball back. Money is external.
He is learning, well behind his desperate eyes,
The epistemology of loss, how to stand up
Knowing what every man must one day know
And most know many days, how to stand up.
And gradually light returns to the street,
20   A whistle blows, the ball is out of sight,
Soon part of me will explore the deep and dark
Floor of the harbour . . . I am everywhere,
I suffer and move, my mind and my heart move
With all that move me, under the water
Or whistling, I am not a little boy.

WALTER M.B. NHLAPO

The *Mendi*

Of many deeds of sacrifice worth a place in history,
Is sinking of the *Mendi* with Africa's dusky glory.
Awhile we remember, 'tis worth a souvenir lest it fall,
As years roll onward, tombs effac'd into oblivion's pall,
When brass monuments decay, still in our hearts ever be room.

Immortal is the *Mendi* until earth passeth in flaming doom,
If deeds obtain lasting record, what glory is in the name
Mendi and her noble contingent? Tell the ages their fame,
How in the sorest hour stood not to gaze and hold their breath,
10   Whilst in the fields of Flanders men charged fire and glaring death.

They repose on the breast of the British sea, ne'er tasted strife,
Which they longingly cherished when they left home, peaceful life!
That they were alive, never would write this poem, they are dead,
We dearly mourn for the blood of our blood, rivers of tears shed!

The tears that suffuse the eyes we cannot withhold from flowing,
When we see widowers and orphans prey to chilly winds blowing,
Nor can we forget when round the bowl of vanished years pass,
                          by the fireside sing,
They're amiss, we sacrificed them as loyalty to our king.

When she sank the fog was dense, you and I were sad that day,
20   We felt something was wrong. That day we recall and kneel and say:
What if they sleep, when their duty be done. He, them ever guide,
He, them remember and know that lie concealed in the tide!
O, cruel sea! the day shall ripe when you the *Mendi* crew must yield,
And may we never forget the heroes in the sea sealed!

p. 250)

67

JOHN FREDERICK NIMS (1914–)

Love Poem

My clumsiest dear, whose hands shipwreck vases,
At whose quick touch all glasses chip and ring,
Whose palms are bulls in china, burs in linen,
And have no cunning with any soft thing
Except all ill-at-ease fidgeting people:
The refugee uncertain at the door
You make at home: deftly you steady
The drunk clambering on his undulant floor.

Unpredictable dear, the taxi drivers' terror,
10   Shrinking from far headlights pale as a dime
Yet leaping before red apoplectic streetcars—
Misfit in any space. And never on time.

A wrench in clocks and the solar system. Only
With words and people and love you move at ease.
In traffic of wit expertly manoeuvre
And keep us, all devotion, at your knees.

Forgetting your coffee spreading on our flannel,
Your lipstick grinning on our coat,
So gayly in love's unbreakable heaven
20   Our souls on glory of spilt bourbon float.

Be with me, darling, early and late. Smash glasses—
I will study wry music for your sake.
For should your hands drop white and empty
All the toys of the world would break.

DYLAN THOMAS (1914—1953)

Fern Hill

Now as I was young and easy under the apple boughs
About the lilting house and happy as the grass was green,
    The night above the dingle starry,
        Time let me hail and climb
     Golden in the heydays of his eyes,
And honoured among wagons I was prince of the apple towns
And once below a time I lordly had the trees and leaves
        Trail with daisies and barley
    Down the rivers of the windfall light.

10   And as I was green and carefree, famous among the barns
About the happy yard and singing as the farm was home,
    In the sun that is young once only,
        Time let me play and be
     Golden in the mercy of his means,
And green and golden I was huntsman and herdsman, the calves
Sang to my horn, the foxes on the hills barked clear and cold,
        And the sabbath rang slowly
    In the pebbles of the holy streams.

All the sun long it was running, it was lovely, the hay
20   Fields high as the house, the tunes from the chimneys, it was air
        And playing, lovely and watery
          And fire green as grass.
        And nightly under the simple stars
As I rode to sleep the owls were bearing the farm away,
All the moon long I heard, blessed among stables, the nightjars
        Flying with the ricks, and the horses
          Flashing into the dark.

And then to awake, and the farm, like a wanderer white
With the dew, come back, the cock on his shoulder: it was all
30   Shining, it was Adam and maiden,
        The sky gathered again
     And the sun grew round that very day.

So it must have been after the birth of the simple light
In the first, spinning place, the spellbound horses walking warm
    Out of the whinnying green stable
        On to the fields of praise.

And honoured among foxes and pheasants by the gay house
Under the new made clouds and happy as the heart was long,
    In the sun born over and over,
40   I ran my heedless ways,
    My wishes raced through the house high hay
And nothing I cared, at my sky blue trades, that time allows
In all his tuneful turning so few and such morning songs
    Before the children green and golden
        Follow him out of grace,

Nothing I cared, in the lamb white days, that time would take me
Up to the swallow thronged loft by the shadow of my hand,
    In the moon that is always rising,
        Nor that riding to sleep
50   I should hear him fly with the high fields
And wake to the farm forever fled from the childless land.
Oh as I was young and easy in the mercy of his means,
        Time held me green and dying
    Though I sang in my chains like the sea.

ROBERT LOWELL (1917–1977)

Memories of West Street and Lepke

Only teaching on Tuesdays, book-worming
in pajamas fresh from the washer each morning,
I hog a whole house on Boston's
'hardly passionate Marlborough Street',
where even the man
scavenging filth in the back alley trash cans,
has two children, a beach wagon, a helpmate,
and is a 'young Republican'.
I have a nine months' daughter,
10   young enough to be my granddaughter.
Like the sun she rises in her flame-flamingo infants' wear.

These are the tranquillized *Fifties*,
and I am forty. Ought I to regret my seedtime?
I was a fire-breathing Catholic C.O.,
and made my manic statement,
telling off the state and president, and then
sat waiting sentence in the bull pen
beside a Negro boy with curlicues
of marijuana in his hair.

20   Given a year,
I walked on the roof of the West Street Jail, a short
enclosure like my school soccer court,
and saw the Hudson River once a day
through sooty clothesline entanglements
and bleaching khaki tenements.
Strolling, I yammered metaphysics with Abramowitz,
a jaundice-yellow ('it's really tan')
and fly-weight pacifist,
so vegetarian,
30   he wore rope shoes and preferred fallen fruit.
He tried to convert Bioff and Brown,
the Hollywood pimps, to his diet.
Hairy, muscular, suburban,
wearing chocolate double-breasted suits,
they blew their tops and beat him black and blue.

I was so out of things, I'd never heard
of the Jehovah's Witnesses.
'Are you a C.O.?' I asked a fellow jailbird.
'No,' he answered, 'I'm a J.W.'
40   He taught me the 'hospital tuck',
and pointed out the T-shirted back
of *Murder Incorporated's* Czar Lepke,
there piling towels on a rack,
or dawdling off to his little segregated cell full
of things forbidden the common man:
a portable radio, a dresser, two toy American
flags tied together with a ribbon of Easter palm.
Flabby, bald, lobotomized,
he drifted in a sheepish calm,
50   where no agonizing reappraisal
jarred his concentration on the electric chair—
hanging like an oasis in his air
of lost connections . . .

(p. 250)

GUY BUTLER (1918–)

Common Dawn

Submitting to a sentry's fate
I concentrate
On the day's way of dawning—

Grey clouds brighten, birds awake,
Wings and singing shake
The curtained silence of the morning.

As gentle as a bird, the breeze
Brushes the grass about my knees
So softly that the dew remains

10   On every blade from here to where
Alien sentries, watching, share
The view of fatal plains.

Alone, awake, I sense how still
Is the presence of a timeless hill,
How universal all this air,

Till I can hardly bear to face
Such sweet and subtle commonplace,
The sunlight everywhere.

The Underdogs

Against the ferro-concrete cliff
Of the Stupendous Cinema,
Behind bright chattering queues of fans,
Motionless, four loafers lean:

Black statues in the flurrying street,
Statues of seamless diorite;
Only their sullen eyes give warning
That such dark stones are dangerous.

You, who think a race will draw your water
10   And wash your dishes and dresses forever and ever,
Who wish they'd stay nice unspoilt kaffirs, forever
Taking your orders on farms and mines,

Look at these rebels! They have renounced
The nice obedience of the sons of Ham,
Have joined, instead, the bitter tribes
Of Ishmael and of Cain.

Look at them. Repulsive, degraded
And coldly self-assured. No glib tongue
Smoothes their speech. They have found
20   A danger-deep integrity. Look!

Terror of White suburbs, smelling of stale skokiaan,
Smoking lipsticked stubs of picked-up cigarettes,
Waiting for night, the burglars' tart,
Waiting for night.

This refusal to be menials,
This devil's pride in pits of crime and fear
Shall cry in crisis like a thunderclap
Through midnight gales of yelling recruits.

Time, surer than the Stock Exchange
30   Will pay big dividends to underdogs:
Injustice, stronger than a Parliament
Will grant red rights to underdogs,

To forget all terror in despair,
To marry violence with hope . . .
So what! We, of the chosen pigmentation,
Shall calmly call on our tribalized God:

'Lord, save the shining Christian culture
Of White South Africa!' Then squat
Heroically behind clean Vickers guns
40   Jabbering death in our innocent hands.

RUTH MILLER (1919–1969)

The Stranger

The light plays tricks upon the senses—
Dense dark things—that can't unlearn
The first lesson, the stern
Reality of the uncorrected vision.

Coming up Cavendish Road, in the late evening, saw
Under a lamp-post, on the lifting corner
His feet set against the flight of the lifting hill—
Bare legs astride—a Japanese Samurai.

In the shadow of the lamp he glares
10   At invisible, invincible legions,
Their teeth bared, flashing curved metal,
Lust in their eyes, salty, bleeding

Ready to flash, move like a snake, sting—
Bring history into the quiet suburban streets
Where the grass grows and the red lilies
Burst like blood.

               Samurai? One would be mad
To think it. Look again: It is only the old
African cleaner, in the late evening, at ease,
20   Slack, quiet, unassuming, his hands resting.

Passers-by flick him with a disregarding glance,
No more acknowledging him than they would
The Samurai in their own blood.

D.J. ENRIGHT (1920–)

The Quagga

By mid-century there were two quaggas left,
And one of the two was male.
The cares of office weighed heavily on him.
When you are the only male of a species,
It is not easy to lead a normal sort of life.

The goats nibbled and belched in casual content;
They charged and skidded up and down their concrete mountain.
One might cut his throat on broken glass,
Another stray too near the tigers.
10   But they were zealous husbands; and the enclosure was always full,
Its rank air throbbing with ingenuous voices.

The quagga, however, was a man of destiny.
His wife, whom he had met rather late in her life,
Preferred to sleep, or complain of the food and the weather.
For their little garden was less than paradisiac,
With its artificial sun that either scorched or left you cold,
And savants with cameras eternally hanging around,
To perpetuate the only male quagga in the world.

Perhaps that was why he failed to do it himself.
20   It is all very well for goats and monkeys—
But the last male of a species is subject to peculiar pressures.
If ancient Satan had come slithering in, perhaps . . .
But instead the savants, with cameras and notebooks,
Writing sad stories of the decadence of quaggas.

And then one sultry afternoon he started raising Cain.
This angry young quagga kicked the bars and broke a camera;
He even tried to bite his astonished keeper.
He protested loud and clear against this and that,
Till the other animals became quite embarrassed
30   For he seemed to be calling them names.

Then he noticed his wife, awake with the noise,
And a curious feeling quivered round his belly.
He was Adam: there was Eve.
Galloping over to her, his head flung back,
He stumbled, and broke a leg, and had to be shot.

Moral Story

On the first professional, Simonides, hangs a tale
Which says that he, at a banquet, was commissioned to sing
Verses in praise of his host for a sum agreed on.
The poet composed a panegyric; recited it all;
But its purchaser appeared dissatisfied with the thing:
The contract had been interpreted with too much freedom.

'Half of your verses are concerned with the Heavenly Pair!
Here, therefore, is half of your fee! If you require a full
Payment, make application to Castor, Pollux, and Co.
10 When poets waste verse on the Gods, I consider it fair
The Gods should condescend to foot their part of the bill.'
Everyone else at table agreed this ought to be so.

It seemed they enjoyed the joke. Before the poet could speak
His mind in words that he might have regretted, a butler
Appeared, to announce two strange gentlemen outside the door,
Who were knocking as if they'd been waiting there for a week,
Asking for Mr Simonides. What could be subtler?
One of them must have been Pollux, and the other, Castor.

Simonides quitted the room to see what they wanted,
20 But barely had he crossed the threshold, than its roof fell in,
And beams squashed the cheat like a cockroach, and everyone else;
The incident left the poet unhurt and enchanted.
But he saw to it that the miracle lost no force in telling,
When, later, he thought any debitor likely to welsh.

The moral of the story is, that philistines should keep
All bargains which they make with artists, and pay up at once.
That is of course perfectly obvious. Nevertheless, any
Poet can point a less evident, if not a more deep,
Moral in this business of Simonides, needing funds,
30 Yet paid by neither the man nor the Gods one penny.

(p. 250)

GABRIEL OKARA (1921–   )

One Night at Victoria Beach

The wind comes rushing from the sea,
the waves curling like mambas strike
the sands and recoiling hiss in rage
washing the Aladuras' feet pressing hard
on the sand and with eyes fixed hard
on what only hearts can see, they shouting
pray, the Aladuras pray; and coming
from booths behind, compelling highlife
forces ears; and car lights startle pairs
10   arm in arm passing washer-words back
and forth like haggling sellers and buyers—

Still they pray, the Aladuras pray
with hands pressed against their hearts
and their white robes pressed against
their bodies by the wind; and drinking
palm-wine and beer, the people boast
at bars at the beach. Still they pray.

They pray, the Aladuras pray
to what only hearts can see while dead
20   fishermen long dead with bones rolling
nibbled clean by nibbling fishes, follow
four dead cowries shining like stars
into deep sea where fishes sit in judgement;
and living fishermen in dark huts
sit round dim lights with Babalawo
throwing their souls in four cowries
on sand, trying to see tomorrow.

Still, they pray, the Aladuras pray
to what only hearts can see behind
30   the curling waves and the sea, the stars
and the subduing unanimity of the sky
and their white bones beneath the sand.

And standing dead on dead sands,
I felt my knees touch living sands—
but the rushing wind killed the budding words.

(p. 250)

Piano and Drums

When at break of day at a riverside
I hear jungle drums telegraphing
the mystic rhythm, urgent, raw
like bleeding flesh, speaking of
primal youth and the beginning,
I see the panther ready to pounce,
the leopard snarling about to leap
and the hunters crouch with spears poised;

And my blood ripples, turns torrent,
10 topples the years and at once I'm
in my mother's laps a suckling;
at once I'm walking simple
paths with no innovations,
rugged, fashioned with the naked
warmth of hurrying feet and groping hearts
in green leaves and wild flowers pulsing.

Then I hear a wailing piano
solo speaking of complex ways
in tear-furrowed concerto;
20 of far away lands
and new horizons with
coaxing diminuendo, counterpoint,
crescendo. But lost in the labyrinth
of its complexities, it ends in the middle
of a phrase at a daggerpoint.

And I lost in the morning mist
of an age at a riverside keep
wandering in the mystic rhythm
of jungle drums and the concerto.

RICHARD WILBUR (1921-)

Playboy

High on his stockroom ladder like a dunce
The stock-boy sits, and studies like a sage
The subject matter of one glossy page,
As lost in curves as Archimedes once.

Sometimes, without a glance, he feeds himself.
The left hand, like a mother-bird in flight,
Brings him a sandwich for a sidelong bite,
And then returns it to a dusty shelf.

What so engrosses him? The wild décor
10   Of this pink-papered alcove into which
A naked girl has stumbled, with its rich
Welter of pelts and pillows on the floor,

Amidst which, kneeling in a supple pose,
She lifts a goblet in her farther hand,
As if about to toast a flower-stand
Above which hovers an exploding rose

Fired from a long-necked crystal vase that rests
Upon a tasselled and vermilion cloth
One taste of which would shrivel up a moth?
20   Or is he pondering her perfect breasts?

Nothing escapes him of her body's grace
Or of her floodlit skin, so sleek and warm
And yet so strangely like a uniform,
But what now grips his fancy is her face,

And how the cunning picture holds her still
At just that smiling instant when her soul,
Grown sweetly faint, and swept beyond control,
Consents to his inexorable will.

(p. 250)

Praise in Summer

Obscurely yet most surely called to praise,
As sometimes summer calls us all, I said
The hills are heavens full of branching ways
Where star-nosed moles fly overhead the dead;
I said the trees are mines in air, I said
See how the sparrow burrows in the sky!
And then I wondered why this mad *instead*
Perverts our praise to uncreation, why
Such savour's in this wrenching things awry.
10   Does sense so stale that it must needs derange
The world to know it? To a praiseful eye
Should it not be enough of fresh and strange
That trees grow green, and moles can course in clay,
And sparrows sweep the ceiling of our day?

To the Etruscan Poets

Dream fluently, still brothers, who when young
Took with your mothers' milk the mother tongue,

In which pure matrix, joining world and mind,
You strove to leave some line of verse behind

Like a fresh track across a field of snow,
Not reckoning that all could melt and go.

(p. 250)

PHILIP LARKIN (1922–1985)

Mr Bleaney

'This was Mr Bleaney's room. He stayed
The whole time he was at the Bodies, till
They moved him.' Flowered curtains, thin and frayed,
Fall to within five inches of the sill,

Whose window shows a strip of building land,
Tussocky, littered. 'Mr Bleaney took
My bit of garden properly in hand.'
Bed, upright chair, sixty-watt bulb, no hook

Behind the door, no room for books or bags—
'I'll take it.' So it happens that I lie
Where Mr Bleaney lay, and stub my fags
On the same saucer-souvenir, and try

Stuffing my ears with cotton-wool, to drown
The jabbering set he egged her on to buy.
I know his habits—what time he came down,
His preference for sauce to gravy, why

He kept on plugging at the four aways—
Likewise their yearly frame: the Frinton folk
Who put him up for summer holidays,
And Christmas at his sister's house in Stoke.

But if he stood and watched the frigid wind
Tousling the clouds, lay on the fusty bed
Telling himself that this was home, and grinned,
And shivered, without shaking off the dread

That how we live measures our own nature,
And at his age having no more to show
Than one hired box should make him pretty sure
He warranted no better, I don't know.

(p. 250)

Next, Please

Always too eager for the future, we
Pick up bad habits of expectancy.
Something is always approaching; every day
Till then we say,

Watching from a bluff the tiny, clear,
Sparkling armada of promises draw near.
How slow they are! And how much time they waste,
Refusing to make haste!

Yet still they leave us holding wretched stalks
Of disappointment, for, though nothing balks
Each big approach, leaning with brasswork prinked,
Each rope distinct,

Flagged, and the figurehead with golden tits
Arching our way, it never anchors; it's
No sooner present than it turns to past.
Right to the last

We think each one will heave to and unload
All good into our lives, all we are owed
For waiting so devoutly and so long.
But we are wrong:

Only one ship is seeking us, a black-
Sailed unfamiliar, towing at her back
A huge and birdless silence. In her wake
No waters breed or break.

HOWARD MOSS (1922–)

Horror Movie

Dr. Unlikely, we love you so,
You who made the double-headed rabbits grow
From a single hare. Mutation's friend,
Who could have prophesied the end
When the Spider Woman deftly snared the fly
And the monsters strangled in a monstrous kiss
And somebody hissed, 'You'll hang for this!'?

Dear Dracula, sleeping on your native soil,
(Any other kind makes him spoil),
10   How we clapped when you broke the French door down
And surprised the bride in the overwrought bed.
Perfectly dressed for lunar research,
Your evening cape added much,
Though the bride, inexplicably dressed in furs,
Was a study in jaded jugulars.

Poor, tortured Leopard Man, you changed your spots
In the debauched village of the Pin-Head Tots;
How we wrung our hands, how we wept
When the eighteenth murder proved inept,
20   And, caught in the Phosphorous Cave of Sea,
Dangling the last of synthetic flesh,
You said, 'There's something wrong with me.'

The Wolf Man knew when he prowled at dawn
Beginnings spin a web where endings spawn.
The bat who lived on shaving cream,
A household pet of Dr. Dream,
Unfortunately, maddened by the bedlam,
Turned on the Doc, bit the hand that fed him.

And you, Dr. X, who killed by moonlight,
30   We loved your scream in the laboratory
When the panel slid and the night was starry
And you threw the inventor in the crocodile pit
(An obscure point: Did he deserve it?)
And you took the gold to Transylvania
Where no one guessed how insane you were.

We thank you for the moral and the mood,
Dear Dr. Cliché, Nurse Platitude.
When we meet again by the Overturned Grave,
Near the Sunken City of the Twisted Mind,
40   (In The Son of the Son of Frankenstein),
Make the blood flow, make the motive muddy:
There's a little death in every body.

AGOSTINHO NETO (1922–1979)

Western Civilisation

Sheets of tin nailed to posts
driven in the ground
make up the house.

Some rags complete
the intimate landscape.

The sun slanting through cracks
welcomes the owner

After twelve hours of slave
labour.

10   breaking rock
shifting rock
breaking rock
shifting rock
fair weather
wet weather
breaking rock
shifting rock

Old age comes early

a mat on dark nights
20   is enough when he dies
gratefully
of hunger.

Angola, 1974
(trans. from the Portuguese)

NISSIM EZEKIEL (1924–)

Night of the Scorpion

I remember the night my mother
was stung by a scorpion. Ten hours
of steady rain had driven him
to crawl beneath a sack of rice.
Parting with his poison—flash
of diabolic tail in the dark room—
he risked the rain again.
The peasants came like swarms of flies
and buzzed the name of God a hundred times
to paralyze the Evil One.
With candles and with lanterns
throwing giant scorpion shadows
on the sun-baked walls
they searched for him: he was not found.
They clicked their tongues.
With every movement that the scorpion made
his poison moved in mother's blood, they said.
May he sit still, they said.
May the sins of your previous birth
be burned away tonight, they said.
May your suffering decrease
the misfortunes of your next birth, they said.
May the sum of evil
balanced in this unreal world
against the sum of good
become diminished by your pain, they said.
May the poison purify your flesh
of desire, and your spirit of ambition,
they said, and they sat around
on the floor with my mother in the centre,
the peace of understanding on each face.
More candles, more lanterns, more neighbours,
more insects, and the endless rain.
My mother twisted through and through
groaning on a mat.

My father, sceptic, rationalist,
trying every curse and blessing,
powder, mixture, herb and hybrid.
He even poured a little paraffin
40   upon the bitten toe and put a match to it.
I watched the flame feeding on my mother.
I watched the holy man perform his rites
to tame the poison with an incantation.
After twenty hours
it lost its sting.

My mother only said
Thank God the scorpion picked on me
and spared my children.

Poet, Lover, Birdwatcher

To force the pace and never to be still
Is not the way of those who study birds
Or women. The best poets wait for words.
The hunt is not an exercise of will
But patient love relaxing on a hill
To note the movement of a timid wing;
Until the one who knows that she is loved
No longer waits but risks surrendering—
In this the poet finds his moral proved,
10   Who never spoke before his spirit moved.

The slow movement seems, somehow, to say much more.
To watch the rarer birds, you have to go
Along deserted lanes and where the rivers flow
In silence near the source, or by a shore
Remote and thorny like the heart's dark floor.
And there the women slowly turn around,
Not only flesh and bone but myths of light
With darkness at the core, and sense is found
By poets lost in crooked, restless flight,
20   The deaf can hear, the blind recover sight.

SYDNEY CLOUTS (1926–1983)

Frog

His onepump
nightfall
youngblood gwawking in the bog—no

prince: all
in reach
small flies gulped once

wild, so
serenely;
nothing out of reach,

10   no excuse, no
magic tightening
his back into the surface of a stone

or log
or frog
or with a leap, into the heartbeat of a man:

man: convex
privacy of chin;
eyes nose mouth turn with it and pause

and haunt the world:
20   the again and the again
at the brink where the waterlilies lie.

'I am not the turtledove
the ringdove, flying,
the sun on the brink, the lion coming down to drink.'

Said, not by him,
not *his* words—Splash!
no millenium: it's his place, it stuck to him,

Lamb-lion of the low mud . . . he's gone.
O bulging eye.

ALLEN GINSBERG (1926–)

In Back of the Real

railroad yard in San Jose
      I wandered desolate
in front of a tank factory
      and sat on a bench
near the switchman's shack.

A flower lay on the hay on
      the asphalt highway
—the dread hay flower
      I thought—It had a
10 brittle black stem and
      corolla of yellowish dirty
spikes like Jesus' inchlong
      crown, and a soiled
dry centre cotton tuft
      like a used shaving brush
that's been lying under
      the garage for a year.

Yellow, yellow flower, and
      flower of industry,
20 tough spikey ugly flower,
      flower nonetheless,
with the form of the great yellow
      Rose in your brain!
This is the flower of the World.

ELIZABETH JENNINGS (1926–)

My Grandmother

She kept an antique shop—or it kept her.
Among Apostle spoons and Bristol glass,
The faded silks, the heavy furniture,
She watched her own reflection in the brass
Salvers and silver bowls, as if to prove
Polish was all, there was no need of love.

And I remember how I once refused
To go out with her, since I was afraid.
It was perhaps a wish not to be used
Like antique objects. Though she never said
That she was hurt, I still could feel the guilt
Of that refusal, guessing how she felt.

Later, too frail to keep a shop, she put
All her best things in one long narrow room,
The place smelt old, of things too long kept shut,
The smell of absences where shadows come
That can't be polished. There was nothing then
To give her own reflection back again.

And when she died I felt no grief at all,
Only the guilt of what I once refused.
I walked into her room among the tall
Sideboards and cupboards—things she never used
But needed; and no finger-marks were there,
Only the new dust falling through the air.

Ghosts

Those houses haunt in which we leave
Something undone. It is not those
Great words or silences of love

That spread their echoes through a place
And fill the locked-up unbreathed gloom.
Ghosts do not haunt with any face

That we have known; they only come
With arrogance to thrust at us
Our own omissions in a room.

10   The words we would not speak they use,
The deeds we dared not act they flaunt,
Our nervous silences they bruise;

It is our helplessness they choose
And our refusals that they haunt.

CHARLES TOMLINSON (1927–)

Paring the Apple

There are portraits and still-lives.

And there is paring the apple.

And then? Paring it slowly,
From under cool-yellow
Cold-white emerging. And . . .?

The spring of concentric peel
Unwinding off white,
The blade hidden, dividing.

There are portraits and still-lives
10 And the first, because 'human'
Does not excel the second, and
Neither is less weighted
With a human gesture, than paring the apple
With a human stillness.

The cool blade
Severs between coolness, apple-rind
Compelling a recognition.

LIONEL ABRAHAMS (1928–)

Half a Week around the New Moon

I wonder about this modern way with demons—
this frank admission that out there
(instead of sheer Otherness,
unthinkable enemy energy)
in the space around each orderly house
blustering like a storm
electric with danger and noisy
with promises that could mean
hell or joy, there's a howling Self
with suggestive eyes and red-stained teeth.
Give him a name, they say:
Mephisto is old hat, but that's the idea—
someone to recognise and deal with:
Demian . . . Daimon . . . My Demon . . .
Libido is eminently suitable . . .
Then open the door and let him in
out of the cold (you'll notice immediately
how the meteorological turbulence subsides),
give him a space in the house.
It's the honest, rational, healthy thing to do.
He's part of you, after all—
after all, you're not all good and pure,
to use an antiquated expression.
His role will be to ensure
that emotions don't go deprived
of salutary stimulation,
he will keep your responses lively,
ensuring at all hours
just that touch of the unpredictable.
And under your eyes he's unlikely
to start a fire or toss the roof off its rafters.

Of course, if you understand his nature
you accept that here has to be
the occasional outing—
the fight, the orgy, the trip—
it's all in the name of balance,
a sane and wholesome development.
But I wonder about this modern way with demons—
should one let them out on Thursdays,
40 or give them half a week around new moon?

(p. 250)

Doctor History Delivers another Political Martyr

History will get you if you don't
(or if you do)
watch out!

Centenarians succumb to the effects
of delaying the inevitable,
but the prisoner aged thirty dies
for the opposite cause: the effects
of bringing on what has to be.

What kills him is the health
10 of History's obstetric process—
advancing the advance of Nemesis
on those his fall leaves clear and cold.
The young man finds a useful end,
a Necessary way to die.

O, Doctor History, we
thank you very much, but
can you mend one
broken brain?

95

Elvis Presley

Two minutes long it pitches through some bar:
Unreeling from a corner box, the sign
Of this one, in his gangling finery
And crawling sideburns, wielding a guitar.

The limitations where he found success
Are ground on which he, panting, stretches out
In turn, promiscuously, by every note,
Our idiosyncrasy and our likeness.

We keep ourselves in touch with a mere dime:
10   Distorting hackneyed words in hackneyed songs
He turns revolt into a style, prolongs
The impulse to a habit of the time.

Whether he poses or is real, no cat
Bothers to say: the pose held is a stance,
Which, generation of the very chance
It wars on, may be posture for combat.

A.K. RAMANUJAN (1929–   )

A River

In Madurai,
        city of temples and poets
who sang of cities and temples:

every summer
a river dries to a trickle
in the sand,
baring the sand-ribs,
straw and women's hair
clogging the watergates
at the rusty bars
under the bridges with patches
of repair all over them,
the wet stones glistening like sleepy
crocodiles, the dry ones
shaven water-buffaloes lounging in the sun.

The poets sang only of the floods.

He was there for a day
when they had the floods.
People everywhere talked
of the inches rising,
of the precise number of cobbled steps
run over by the water, rising
on the bathing places,
and the way it carried off three village houses,
one pregnant woman
and a couple of cows
named Gopi and Brinda, as usual.

The new poets still quoted
the old poets, but no one spoke
in verse
of the pregnant woman
drowned, with perhaps twins in her,
kicking at blank walls
even before birth.

He said:
the river has water enough
to be poetic
about only once a year
and then
40   it carries away
in the first half-hour
three village houses,
a couple of cows
named Gopi and Brinda
and one pregnant woman
expecting identical twins
with no moles on their bodies,
with different-coloured diapers

to tell them apart.

(p. 251)

JAMES MATTHEWS (1929–)

They Say

they say
writing poetry at
this stage of
our struggle is
absurd, and writing
black protest poetry
is even worse
people need direction
and not words
10   relating the situation
as it is
things that everyone
knows all about
poets, black poets,
have written themselves
into a dead-end

they say
my neighbours do
not even read
20   what i've written
and that poetry
will not bring
about any changes
in our situation
a revolution can
do without poets
poets should switch to
things more constructive
furthering a revolution
30   offer a solution
to the problem
their contempt
is acid eating
the flesh of
my poetical work

(1981)

TED HUGHES (1930–)

Snowdrop

Now is the globe shrunk tight
Round the mouse's dulled wintering heart.
Weasel and crow, as if moulded in brass,
Move through an outer darkness
Not in their right minds,
With the other deaths. She, too, pursues her ends,
Brutal as the stars of this month,
Her pale head heavy as metal.

Crow's First Lesson

God tried to teach Crow how to talk.
'Love,' said God. 'Say, Love.'
Crow gaped, and the white shark crashed into the sea
And went rolling downwards, discovering its own depth.

'No, no,' said God, 'Say Love. Now try it. LOVE.'
Crow gaped, and a bluefly, a tsetse, a mosquito
Zoomed out and down
To their sundry flesh-pots.

'A final try,' said God. 'Now, LOVE.'
10   Crow convulsed, gaped, retched and
Man's bodiless prodigious head
Bulbed out onto the earth, with swivelling eyes,
Jabbering protest—

And Crow retched again, before God could stop him.
And woman's vulva dropped over man's neck and tightened.
The two struggled together on the grass.
God struggled to part them, cursed, wept—

Crow flew guiltily off.

The Thought-Fox

I imagine this midnight moment's forest:
Something else is alive
Beside the clock's loneliness
And this blank page where my fingers move.

Through the window I see no star:
Something more near
Though deeper within darkness
Is entering the loneliness:

Cold, delicately as the dark snow,
A fox's nose touches twig, leaf;
Two eyes serve a movement, that now
And again now, and now, and now

Sets neat prints into the snow
Between trees, and warily a lame
Shadow lags by stump and in hollow
Of a body that is bold to come

Across clearings, an eye,
A widening deepening greenness,
Brilliantly, concentratedly,
Coming about its own business

Till, with a sudden sharp hot stink of fox
It enters the dark hole of the head.
The window is starless still; the clock ticks,
The page is printed.

PATRICK CULLINAN (1932–)

Exiles

We shall try not to remember
The politics, the quarter truths
That made a total truth to us.
We shall try to remember our own
Temptation, when we had the power
And used it; when we had
It like a handkerchief
In the corner of our sleeves.
And if there was something absurd
10 About tennis on the equator,
It was the absurdity we drowned
With long drinks in the evening.

It is true: they have a personality.
But not, it seems, the one we saw.
Can any race have two
Personalities? There is something
Mad about facts when they diverge.
We remember what we saw. We knew them.
We knew them well enough to want their good.
20 And now we talk too much about it,
The dialects bore our countrymen,
Words that once meant boy or farm
Irritate our flesh and blood.

We are easily forgotten
By them. Could they have done better?
For there was one thing we ourselves
Could not understand.
We were native from the start,
With brown bush and the blue
30 Mountains, from the first moment
With wood smoke at dawn
That no one can describe, the birds,
The sticky heat we grew to love.
We thought we were exiles,
We are certainly exiles now.

The worst lie was our hope:
Perpetual teatime and the colour green.
Fantasies always suffice
But we returned to the lie,
40   The dirty towns, the insensitive people,
Endless teatime and the colour green.
But we can forgive this remembering
One promise: driving through
Long grass at night, the scratch
Of the grass on the truck,
And in our headlights a continent,
An Africa within. An Africa beyond.

Wind on the Half-Moon

That was not the way to you,
crossing the great bridge:
had you wished it I would have come,
navigating drains and sewers:
but the sun flashed on the verandah windows
and by then I had lost my strength.

'Tell me,' said the man preaching on the crescent,
'do you know where God is?'
I knew so I told him.
10   He shook his head and went on the wind that rushed,
that lifted men and houses into the sky,
into the blackness of pitch.

(after Eugenio Montale)

DOUGLAS LIVINGSTONE (1932–)

One Elephant

About that time arose one elephant
from all the herd who stopped and cleared his throat
and said: I can't for all the world at all
remember what it was I had to say;
I only know it was of great importance.

He shook his ears; looked puzzled; slapped himself
with gusto on the back and raised the dust;
shifted capacious businessman's hindquarters
in their ill-fitting pants; harrumphed and glared
10   at the innocent thorntrees—his audience.

Ah yes! There comes a time when one commits,
despite oneself, the ultimate! And sick
of selfish beasts, their egos and their stench,
their cunning cruelty, destructivity,
one turns, despite oneself, grimly to Man.

Don't you agree? The thorntrees held their peace.
Injured; his tusks aching in their ivory
tower, he wheeled and shambled off to rejoin
the ambling herd, remembering to avoid
20   the smoky nests of heedless tingling ants.

The Zoo Affair

With some it is water shrugging, bunched and oily
at the quayside—the cold welcome of lewd carpets;
for others, the pineal-sucked lure, dragging dizzy
and out from windy skyscraper parapets.

With him it was the tiger: beautifully slack;
indifferent; sleep and captivity thinned;
lying on a fat pole like a striped rug, back-
legs adangle, forepaws crossed under chin.

He even learnt a few words of Bengali (culled
10   from Tagore) and leapt the ditch to press
      long and urgently at the bars, mad to scratch unpulled,
      tortoise-shelled and round furry ears.

      Angry keepers and others ordered him back and he
      went, backwards, arms out, aching and bent
      about air the size of a tiger, and thought of his granite-
      faced and quite unfurry apartment.

      To shed his love one night he broke in, sat his
      city trousers a moment on a foliage-crusted stone wall,
      jumped running for the beloved bars, fumbled latches
20   and reverently entered the shrine through the feed-door.

      For perhaps one second he felt it, face buried in rank
      cat's fur: the sleepy response. Then the rasped purr
      meshed with metallic springs. The barrelling flanks
      pumped an outraged blast from alien vaults of power.

      They found him on the floor early next morning, his head
      a split and viscid watermelon; loosely the wet tufts
      of combed brains spilled, his smile quiet through the red;
      beside him, for warmth, the cosy sprawl of his love.

(p. 251)

Sonatina of Peter Govender, Beached

Sometime busdriver
of *Shiva's Pride, The Off-Course Tote,*
The Venus Trap and *The Khyber Pass Express*.
I've fathered five bright, beguiling,
alert-eyed but gill-less children.
I had to fish:
first, surf; then the blue-water marlin.
(I heard a Man once
walked water without getting wet.)
10   Old duels for fares:
The South Coast road—all we could get;
my left hand conning the wheel.

My last was *Dieselene Conqueror*
—night-muggings, cops,
knives, that coked and jammed injector
—right hand nursing in me a reel,
the cane cracking at the start of the day,
things of the land becoming remote.
My prime as oarsman:
20   heroics of the offshore boat,
catching all that steel slabs of sea could express.
My porpoise-wife is gone, seeded,
spent, queen among curry-makers.
I'm old now, curt.

I've monosyllables for strangers
who stop by asking
questions while I repair my net.
Things learnt from the sea
—gaffing the landlord, the week's debt,
30   scooping in the crazed white shads,
twisting the great transparent mountains
past a wood blade—?
Contempt for death is the hard-won
ultimate, the only freedom
(—cracking the cane at the end of the day—):
not one of the men I knew could float.

CHRISTOPHER OKIGBO (1932–1967)

Come Thunder

Now that the triumphant march has entered the last street
    corners,
Remember, O dancers, the thunder among the clouds . . .

Now that the laughter, broken in two, hangs tremulous between
    the teeth,
Remember, O dancers, the lightning beyond the earth . . .

The smell of blood already floats in the lavender-mist of the
    afternoon.
The death sentence lies in ambush along the corridors of power;
And a great fearful thing already tugs at the cables of the open
    air,
A nebula immense and immeasurable, a night of deep waters—
An iron dream unnamed and unprintable, a path of stone.

10   The drowsy heads of the pods in barren farmlands witness it,
    The homesteads abandoned in this century's brush fire witness it:
    The myriad eyes of deserted corn cobs in burning barns witness
        it:
    Magic birds with the miracle of lightning flash on their feathers . . .

    The arrows of God tremble at the gates of light,
    The drums of curfew pander to a dance of death;

    And the secret thing in its heaving
    Threatens with iron mask
    The last lighted torch of the century . . .

(p. 251)

LENRIE PETERS (1932–   )

Homecoming

The present reigned supreme
    Like the shallow floods over the gutters
Over the raw paths where we had been,
    The house with the shutters.

Too strange the sudden change
    Of the times we buried when we left
The times before we had properly arranged
    The memories that we kept.

Our sapless roots have fed
10   The wind-swept seedlings of another age.
Luxuriant weeds have grown where we led
    The Virgins to the water's edge.

There at the edge of the town
    Just by the burial ground
Stands the house without a shadow
    Lived in by new skeletons.

That is all that is left
    To greet us on the homecoming
After we have paced the world
20   And longed for returning.

SYLVIA PLATH (1932–1963)

Mushrooms

Overnight, very
Whitely, discreetly,
Very quietly

Our toes, our noses
Take hold on the loam,
Acquire the air.

Nobody sees us,
Stops us, betrays us;
The small grains make room.

10   Soft fists insist on
Heaving the needles,
The leafy bedding,

Even the paving.
Our hammers, our rams,
Earless and eyeless,

Perfectly voiceless,
Widen the crannies,
Shoulder through holes. We

20   Diet on water,
On crumbs of shadow,
Bland-mannered, asking

Little or nothing.
So many of us!
So many of us!

We are shelves, we are
Tables, we are meek,
We are edible,

Nudgers and shovers
In spite of ourselves.
30   Our kind multiplies:

We shall by morning
Inherit the earth
Our foot's in the door.

Morning Song

Love set you going like a fat gold watch.
The midwife slapped your footsoles, and your bald cry
Took its place among the elements.

Our voices echo, magnifying your arrival. New statue.
In a drafty museum, your nakedness
Shadows our safety. We stand round blankly as walls.

I'm no more your mother
Than the cloud that distils a mirror to reflect its own slow
Effacement at the wind's hand.

10   All night your moth-breath
Flickers among the flat pink roses. I wake to listen:
A far sea moves in my ear.

One cry, and I stumble from bed, cow-heavy and floral
In my Victorian nightgown.
Your mouth opens clean as a cat's. The window square

Whitens and swallows its dull stars. And now you try
Your handful of notes;
The clear vowels rise like balloons.

SIPHO SEPAMLA (1932–   )

To Whom It May Concern

Bearer
Bare of everything but particulars
Is a Bantu
The language of a people in southern Africa
He seeks to proceed from here to there
Please pass him on
Subject to these particulars
He lives
Subject to the provisions
10   Of the Urban Natives Act of 1925
Amended often
To update it to his sophistication
Subject to the provisions of the said Act
He may roam freely within a prescribed area
Free only from the anxiety of conscription
In terms of the Abolition of Passes Act
A latter-day amendment
In keeping with moon-age naming
Bearer's designation is Reference number 417181
20   And (he) acquires a niche in the said area
As a temporary sojourner
To which he must betake himself
At all times
When his services are dispensed with for the day
As a permanent measure of law and order
Please note
The remains of R/N 417181
Will be laid to rest in peace
On a plot
30   Set aside for Methodist Xhosas
A measure also adopted
At the express request of the Bantu
In anticipation of any faction fight
Before the Day of Judgement.

ANTHONY THWAITE (1932–)

Called For

Tonight we drive back late from talk and supper
Across miles of unlit roads, flat field and fen,
Towards home; but on the way must make a detour
And rescue you from what, half-laughingly,
We think of as your temporary world—
Some group or other, all outlandishly
Named and rigged up in fancy dress and loud
With adolescent grief. Well, we're too old
For alien caperings like that. The road
10 Runs towards home and habit, milk and bed.

That unborn child I locked up in neat stanzas
Survives in two or three anthologies,
An effigy sealed off from chance or changes.
Now I arrive near midnight, but too early
To claim you seventeen years afterwards:
A darkened auditorium, lit fitfully
By dizzy crimsons, pulsing and fading blues
Through which electric howls and snarled-out words
Isolate you (though only in my eyes)
20 Sitting among three hundred sprawling bodies.

Your pale face for a second looms up through
The jerking filters, splatterings of colour
As if spawned by the music, red and blue
Over and over—there, your face again,
Not seeing me, not seeing anything,
Distinct and separate, suddenly plain
Among so many others, strangers. Smoke
Lifts as from a winter field, obscuring
All but your face, consuming, as I look,
30 That child I gave protective rhetoric.

Not just this place, the tribal lights, the passive
Communion of noise and being young,
Not just the strident music which I give
No more than half an ear to; but the sense
Of drifting out into another plane
Beyond the one I move on, and moved once
To bring you into being—that is why
I falter as I call you by your name,
Claim you, as drifting up towards me now
40   You smile at me, ready for us to go.

WOLE SOYINKA (1934–   )

Telephone Conversation

The price seemed reasonable, location
Indifferent. The landlady swore she lived
Off premises. Nothing remained
But self-confession. 'Madam', I warned,
'I hate a wasted journey—I am African.'
Silence. Silenced transmission of
Pressurized good-breeding. Voice, when it came,
Lipstick coated, long gold-rolled
Cigarette-holder pipped. Caught I was, foully.
10 'How dark?' . . . I had not misheard . . . 'Are you light
Or very dark?' Button B. Button A. Stench
Of rancid breath of public hide-and-speak.
Red booth. Red pillar-box. Red double-tiered
Omnibus squelching tar. It *was* real! Shamed
By ill-mannered silence, surrender
Pushed dumbfoundment to beg simplification.
Considerate she was, varying the emphasis—
'Are you dark? Or very light?' Revelation came.
'You mean—like plain or milk chocolate?'
20 Her assent was clinical, crushing in its light
Impersonality. Rapidly, wave-length adjusted,
I chose. 'West African sepia'—and as afterthought,
'Down in my passport.' Silence for spectroscopic
Flight of fancy, till truthfulness clanged her accent
Hard on the mouthpiece. 'What's that?' conceding
'Don't know what that is.' 'Like brunette.'
'That's dark, isn't it?' 'Not altogether.
Facially, I am brunette, but madam, you should see
The rest of me. Palm of my hand, soles of my feet
30 Are a peroxide blonde. Friction, caused—
Foolishly madam—by sitting down, has turned
My bottom raven black—One moment madam!'—sensing
Her receiver rearing on the thunderclap
About my ears—'Madam', I pleaded, 'wouldn't you rather
See for youself?'

D.L.P. YALI-MANISI (1936–)

To the Pupils of Nathaniel Nyalusa High School, Grahamstown, 13 June 1979

I greet you, men and young women!
When we're here we're at the village of the son of Rhodes,
A child of Scotsmen,
A child of Englishmen.
They're the vast throngs of Nonibe,
Ones who left England and made a beeline,
And cleaved the water of the sea,
And suddenly they popped up
At *Gqumeliselwandle* of Rharhabe;
10 They cut straight across the land of Phalo,
And entered *Gqumeliphezulu* of the son of Phalo;
We refer to Grahamstown, below the Mount of Sins.

There then's this village of the throngs of Nonibe,
There then's this village of the English,
Whose ears gleam like the sun;
They're called the hungry ones although they've fed,
For though they've eaten butter and bread
Their stomachs have puckered up
And the stomach's met up with the spine;
20 For these men eat not to fill themselves
But they eat to feed their minds.
That's why we see the village of Rhodes
That's why we see the village of the son of the English
Growing to a city far larger
Than the township where the blacks dwell.

Oh these English people, they are blessed!
Oh these English people, they make things which are manifest!
Oh these English people, they know how to set things in order!
For they place education in front.
30 And rely on the Eternal One.

So then, beautiful girls of Phalo's village!
So then, handsome fellows of Rharhabe's country!
Sons of those who spurned flight,
Sons of wearers of ivory arm-rings,
Sons of heroes,

This land of Phalo's in trouble,
For the English grabbed it with cannon and breechloader,
Yet your fathers fought with spear and assegai;
That's why we're scattered and destitute
40   In the land of our ancestors.
But the time for sitting on our rumps is past,
Dropping into rivers, scaling outcrops,
Roaming over cliffs,
Running in futility and hiding away
In clefts that are the haunt of pythons,
For we flee familiarity with the cannon
Which shatters and scatters us,
Which tumbles and butchers us.
So today we tell you the time's at hand
50   To seize your weapons, men,
To take the road we must travel,
Which will offer us that power
That other nations have attained,
Especially the nation of the Englishmen
Who violated the land of Phalo and of Tshiwo

It's you then, young ones of Rharhabe's village,
Seize your weapons and follow the grandson of Sebe,
Seize your weapons and follow the grandson of Maqoma,
Seize your weapons and follow the grandson of Ncamashe,
60   Seize your weapons and know you are Rharhabe's people,
You are the family of Sandile's place,
You are the family of Ngqika's place,
You are the family of Mlawu's place,
There then's your chief at Mngqesha,
He's called Maxhobandile,
But I say nothing, for he's still a child.
We expect him to join up with you
So that you flock to him
And mature with him in education,
70   So that he leads the nation in orderly ranks,
So that he leads the nation with a clear mind:
Oh a nation of dummies
Is the plaything of nations with knowledge!
                I disappear!

(trans. from the Xhosa)

(p. 251)

216

SEAMUS HEANEY (1939—)

Follower

My father worked with a horse-plough,
His shoulders globed like a full sail strung
Between the shafts and the furrow.
The horses strained at his clicking tongue.

An expert. He would set the wing
And fit the bright steel-pointed sock.
The sod rolled over without breaking.
And the headrig, with a single pluck

Of reins, the sweating team turned round
And back into the land. His eye
Narrowed and angled at the ground,
Mapping the furrow exactly.

I stumbled in his hob-nailed wake,
Fell sometimes on the polished sod;
Sometimes he rode me on his back
Dipping and rising to his plod.

I wanted to grow up and plough,
To close one eye, stiffen my arm.
All I ever did was follow
In his broad shadow round the farm.

I was a nuisance, tripping, falling,
Yapping always. But today
It is my father who keeps stumbling
Behind me, and will not go away.

WOPKO JENSMA (1939–   )

Once Rhymes

1

why then can a man
whose heart has been cut out
not grow a new heart?

    my picture of a glass vase
    is hung with ivy and ribbons
    is filled with hearts adrift

cause your guilt is a plant
that yellows in darkness
grows towards the crevice
10   without hope of reaching it

    the vase stands in the middle
    of the table that is laid

2

by the law of our country
a plant was found guilty

the sentence was carried out
before the assembled people

it was first stripped of fear
and then hung by its conscience

the children sang a sweet song
20   and pressed leaves in textbooks

Pullin Strong at Eleven-Forty-Five

1

till mornin an eevnin peewee'n malombo jazz
oh gee boys, who's dat man dere
blow a flute boy
you's my kinda guy—oh hea'm
his byebye baby any monday walkin a ol blues

as jimmy rushing says: any monday 'n
she aint your girl, she aint my girl

no, she's anybody's goddamn girl—an i get
maself ma shootin rod
an slash anybody's skull open
hea me ova, yea hea me
blowin dat lo spiky blues ova
ma dea woman—yea 't aint your beloved ol

downtown orlando: it's solid hearin, you ablo
in a shack oozin. man, feel dat dirge, oh yeya

2

sittin here figure 'n ma gal sure is bad
in passion
in fashion
i killed her. sad she's now dead
i dream bloodhound
on my track, rope round ma neck—
ol hangman grin an
tightens da noose up. wonder who
gonna celebrate ma
death. murders are da lone river
wanderin thru over
yonder
a lord
sittin
chewin
a bit o' sweetreed
i wonder if he knows what it's like man

to be
an in
da sump of a night

3

ma struttin babe, way up—
ma legs
slowly shuffle
into da
40   beat. ma babe—
dey guttin you
eh? come mama, me be da o
daddy—o
a babe, a babe, ma o' love
ma jerk
shine a
city lights, a holy roll:
bust ma
head o'
50   da wall
babe, you stay da smear—
a bit o' dirt
o' gutterdoor
oh, Lord
open up
your door, i'm a comin in

JOHN LENNON (1940–1980) and
PAUL McCARTNEY (1942–)

Eleanor Rigby

Ah, look at all the lonely people!
Ah, look at all the lonely people!

Eleanor Rigby
Picks up the rice in the church where a wedding has been,
Lives in a dream,
Waits at the window
Wearing the face that she keeps in a jar by the door.
Who is it for?

All the lonely people,
Where do they all come from?
All the lonely people,
Where do they all belong?

Father McKenzie,
Writing the words of a sermon that no one will hear,
No one comes near,
Look at him working,
Darning his socks in the night when there's nobody there.
What does he care?

All the lonely people (etc.)

Eleanor Rigby
Died in the church and was buried along with her name,
Nobody came.
Father McKenzie,
Wiping the dirt from his hands as he walks from the grave,
No one was saved.

All the lonely people (etc.)

Ah, look at all the lonely people!
Ah, look at all the lonely people!

MBUYISENI OSWALD MTSHALI (1940–)

An Old Man in Church

I know an old man
who during the week is a machine working at full throttle:
productivity would stall,
spoil the master's high profit estimate,
if on Sunday he did not go to church
to recharge his spiritual batteries.

He never says his prayer in a velvet-cushioned pew—
it would only be a whisper on God's ear.
He falls on raw knees
10   that smudge the bare floor with his piety.
He hits God's heart with screams as hard as stones
flung from the slingshot of his soul.
He takes the gilded communion plate with gnarled hands,
he lowers his eyes into the deep pond of serenity,
his brow rippling with devotion,
his ears enraptured by rustling silk vestments of the priest.
He drinks the Lord's blood from a golden chalice
with cracked lips thirsty for peace.

The acolyte comes around with a brass-coated collection plate:
20   the old man sneaks in a cent piece
that raises a scowl on the collector's face
whose puckered nose sneezes at such poor generosity
instead of inhaling the aromatic incense smoke.
Then the preacher stands up in the pulpit,
his voice fiery with holy fervour:
'Blessed are the meek for they shall inherit the earth.'

STEPHEN GRAY (1941–)

Mayfair

O suburb of stripped cars & highrise hollyhocks
    where the greater unemployed
swat sweat that crawls like flies down fallen legs
    where cataracted chickens gawp
from turning spits in Costa's Terminus Cafe
    where housewives vie on volume
down a one-way street flushed with soap-opera
    & their potato-fat serving girls
shine the Dandy polish on their red knees

backyard archaeology turns up a shard
    plastic rattles glass coal
& the condensed milk throat of the neighbour's
    bat-eared military son
breaks all siesta on his A minor bugle practice
    the jackpot days are over for
the Dixi Cola pensioners in the Thursday
    post-office payout queue
decay like rope around their contoured necks

the mother's clinic scrapes a formless arm with vaccine
    tetanus is in the wind
scabby wild cats track their corrugated clawy paths
    to the bins of the Limosin Hotel
& miners from Frelimo stroll in unofficial gangs
    against the menace of stick em up & defence
& trespass on the Gaza Strip where Reggie and Honey
    packing through Majestic Mansions
deny all knowledge all involvement in crime

down the plane-tree Ninth Avenue rides a blue nun
    on a cross-barred bicycle
down the brick of the Dolphin Street swimming pool
    loiter kids held up by candy floss
down the intersection bounce Clover Dairies ice cream
    sidecars & bells of appetite
down the coach-house whitewash plunge rust and creeper
    & the ritual taxi ride to church
rounds a Pentecostal Sunday curve towards heaven

O Mayfair & a Chinaman's chest flat as a slime-tray
      parades the verandas of concrete wagon wheels
how uplifting!—the pumpkins on roofs still
40   the TRG car come for southern flesh
& Mr Fonseca Builder unclasps his racing pigeons
      to spiral over smallness & the dumps
the fine golden sand the cyanide lagoon the synagogue
      the alcoholic pavements & knives & curlers
into undefeated clarity of the whitest air.

(p. 251)

Sunflower

Poor sunflower, your
neck so stretched and
drooping to your feet

can't see the mossies
can't see your own
glory reflected around

sentenced to death
dropping seed in plastic
bags, it's all over

10   like the hanged man
Pretoria Central
Wednesday dawn.

PETER STRAUSS (1941–   )

The Iron Lung

The cooked earth in the garden
Is almost done. It is an oven.

Going into this garden with the children
I have—(more than tasted)—lived
A kind of peace
That has no meaning for past or future
Or what it means to be an adult.

The roses are rigid.
Burnt into cardboard while still a bud.

If I tell that boy,
He will climb into the trees
And throw down oranges for us.

Taps silver and drip,
Smelling of lime.
The water is black
In cylinders of rust.

My right to be here
Is having been, as a boy, in another such garden,
Kept by another such grandmother.

Meanwhile
From the edges there is this sound
Of a heavy rubber balloon filling and emptying,
A hoarse whistle of pines,
Monotone and arresting.
Keeping things going on the big plain.

City Johannesburg

This way I salute you:
My hand pulses to my back trousers pocket
Or into my inner jacket pocket
For my pass, my life,
Jo'burg City.
My hand like a starved snake rears my pockets
For my thin, ever lean wallet,
While my stomach groans a friendly smile to hunger,
Jo'burg City.
10   My stomach also devours coppers and papers
Don't you know?
Jo'burg City, I salute you;
When I run out, or roar in a bus to you,
I leave behind me, my love,
My comic houses and people, my dongas and my ever whirling dust
My death
That's so related to me as a wink to the eye.
Jo'burg City
I travel on your black and white and roboted roads
20   Through your thick iron breath that you inhale
At six in the morning and exhale from five noon.
Jo'burg City
That is the time when I come to you,
When your neon flowers flaunt from your electrical wind,
That is the time when I leave you,
When your neon flowers flaunt their way through the falling
    darkness
On your cement trees.
And as I go back, to my love,
My dongas, my dust, my people, my death,
30   Where death lurks in the dark like a blade in the flesh,
I can feel your roots, anchoring your might, my feebleness
In my flesh, in my mind, in my blood,
And everything about you says it,
That, that is all you need of me.

Jo'burg City, Johannesburg,
Listen when I tell you,
There is no fun, nothing, in it,
When you leave the women and men with such frozen expressions,
Expressions that have tears like furrows of soil erosion,
40 Jo'burg City, you are dry like death,
Jo'burg City, Johannesburg, Jo'burg City.

The Actual Dialogue

Do not fear Baas.
It's just that I appeared
And our faces met
In this black night that's like me.
Do not fear—
We will always meet
When you do not expect me.
I will appear
In the night that's black like me.
10 Do not fear—
Blame your heart
When you fear me—
I will blame my mind
When I fear you
In the night that's black like me.
Do not fear Baas,
My heart is vast as the sea
And your mind as the earth.
It's awright Baas,
20 Do not fear.

JENNIFER DAVIDS (1945–)

Poem for my Mother

That isn't everything, you said
on the afternoon I brought a poem
to you hunched over the washtub
with your hands
the shrivelled
burnt granadilla
skin of your hands
covered by foam.

And my words
10   slid like a ball
of hard blue soap
into the tub
to be grabbed and used by you
to rub the clothes.

A poem isn't all
there is to life, you said
with your blue-ringed gaze
scanning the page
once looking over my shoulder
20   and back at the immediate
dirty water

and my words
being clenched
smaller and
smaller.

MAFIKA GWALA (1946–   )

The Children of Nonti

Nonti Nzimande died long, long ago
Yet his children still live.
Generation after generation, they live on;
Death comes to the children of Nonti
And the children of Nonti cry but won't panic
And there is survival in the children of Nonti.

Poverty swoops its deathly wings. But tough,
strong and witty are the children of Nonti.
The wet rains fall. The roads become like
the marshed rice paddies of the Far East;
And on these desolate roads there is song
Song in the Black voices of the children of Nonti.

Someone marries
The bride does not hide her face under the veil;
The maidens dance near the kraal
Dance before the 'make it be merry' eyes
of the elders. The elders joshing it
on their young days.
There is still free laughter
in the children of Nonti.

An ox drops to the earth, then another;
Knives run into the meat. Making the feast
to be bloodfilled with Life.
The old, the dead, are brought into the Present
of continuous nature in the children of Nonti
Got to be a respecting with the children of Nonti.

When a daughter has brought shame
The women show anger; not wrath.
And the illegitimate born is one of
the family.
When a son is charged by the white law
The children of Nonti bring their heads together
In a bid to free one of the children of Nonti.

There are no sixes and nines be one
with the children of Nonti. Truth is truth
and lies are lies amongst the children of Nonti.
For when summer takes its place after the winter
The children of Nonti rejoice
and call it proof of Truth
40   Truth reigns amongst the children of Nonti.

Sometimes a son rises above the others
of the children of Nonti. He explains the workings
and the trappings of white thinking.
The elders debate;
And add to their abounding knowledge
of black experience.
The son is still one of the black children of Nonti
For there is oneness in the children of Nonti.

And later, later when the sun
50   is like forever down;
Later when the dark rules
above the light of Truth
The black children of Nonti will rise and speak.
They will speak of the time
when Nonti lived in peace with his children;
Of the times when age did not count
above experience. The children of Nonti will stand
their grounds in the way that Nonti speared his foes
to free his black brothers from death and woes;
60   They shall fight with the tightened grip
of a cornered pard. For they shall be knowing that
Nothing is more vital than standing up
For the Truths that Nonti lived for.
Then there shall be Freedom in that stand
by the children of Nonti.
Truthful tales shall be told
Of how the children of Nonti pushed their will;
And continued to live by the peace
The peace that Nonti once taught to them.

(p. 251)

CHARLES MUNGOSHI (1947–)

If you don't stay bitter and angry for too long

If you don't stay bitter
and angry for too long
you might finally salvage
something useful
from the old country

a lazy half sleep summer afternoon
for instance; with the whoof-whoof
of grazing cattle in your ears
tails swishing, flicking flies away
or the smell of newly-turned soil
with birds hopping about
in the wake of the plough
in search of worms

or the pained look of your father
a look that took you all these years
and lots of places to understand

the bantering tone you used with your
grandmother and their old laugh
that said nothing matters but death

If you don't stay bitter
and angry for too long
and have the courage to go back
you will discover that the autumn smoke
writes different more hopeful messages
in the high skies of the old country.

Zimbabwe

NJABULO SIMAKAHLE NDEBELE (1948–   )

The Revolution of the Aged

my voice is the measure of my life
it cannot travel far now,
small mounds of earth already bead my open grave,
so come close
    lest you miss the dream.

grey hair has placed on my brow
the verdict of wisdom
and the skin-folds of age
bear tales wooled in the truth of proverbs:
10   if you cannot master the wind,
flow with it
letting know all the time that you are resisting.

that is how i have lived
quietly
swallowing both the fresh and foul
from the mouth of my masters;
yet i watched and listened.

i have listened too
to the condemnations of the young
20   who burned with scorn
    loaded with revolutionary maxims
        hot for quick results.

they did not know
that their anger
was born in the meekness
with which i whipped myself:
it is a blind progeny
that acts without indebtedness to the past.

listen now,
30   the dream:
i was playing music on my flute
when a man came and asked to see my flute
and i gave it to him,
but he took my flute and walked away.
i followed this man, asking for my flute;
he would not give it back to me.
how i planted vegetables in his garden!
   cooked his food!
how i cleaned his house!
40   how i washed his clothes
   and polished his shoes!
but he would not give me back my flute,
yet in my humiliation
i felt the growth of strength in me
for i had a goal
as firm as life is endless,
while he lived in the darkness of his wrong.

now he has grown hollow from the grin of his cruelty
he hisses death through my flute
0   which has grown heavy, too heavy
for his withered hands,
and now i should smite him:
in my hand is the weapon of youth.

do not eat an unripe apple
its bitterness is a tingling knife.
suffer yourself to wait
and the ripeness will come
and the apple will fall down at your feet.

now is the time
   pluck the apple
and feed the future with its ripeness.

CHRIS MANN (1948–   )

Naturalists

The naturalists I know
have brown arms and green thumbs,
and butterflies roost in their beards.
With tiny pads, they wipe polluted dew
from tender throats, and when they sneeze
they pollinate peaches and plums.

Without their patient passion
I wouldn't know why whales
yodel and bloop beneath the sea,
10   how wasps preserve their infant's bully-beef
inside a mud-walled tin, what slopes
to sow, and when to let them sleep.

Molecules and galaxies
swirl and erupt
in universes beyond their focus.
They find enough to live by in between.

In addition to a bee
its pollen pantaloons;
not just a green and russet oak,
20   a thousand pages of philosophy;
more than a vine, a rustling church
transmuting sun and earth to seed.

Quarrels and conquests
swirl and erupt
in universes beyond their focus.
They find enough to marvel at between.

JEREMY CRONIN (1949–   )

To learn how to speak

To learn how to speak
With the voices of the land,
To parse the speech in its rivers,
To catch in the inarticulate grunt,
Stammer, call, cry, babble, tongue's knot
A sense of the stoneness of these stones
From which all words are cut.
To trace with the tongue wagon-trails
Saying the suffix of their aches in -kuil, -pan, -fontein,
In watery names that confirm
The dryness of their ways.
To visit the places of occlusion, or the lick
in a vlei-bank dawn.
To bury my mouth in the pit of your arm,
In that planetarium,
Pectoral beginning to the nub of time
Down there close to the water-table, to feel
The full moon as it drums
At the back of my throat
Its cow-skinned vowel.
To write a poem with words like:
I'm telling you,
Stompie, stickfast, golovan,
Songololo, just boombang, just
To understand the least inflections,
To voice without swallowing
Syllables born in tin shacks, or catch
the 5.15 ikwata bust fife
Chwannisberg train, to reach
The low chant of the mine gang's
Mineral glow of our people's unbreakable resolve.

To learn how to speak
With the voices of this land.

SHABBIR BANOOBHAI (1949–   )

by your own definition

by your own definition
i drink too deeply
the blood of roses

      lean on a leaf
      for comfort

      mistake mysteriously
      a thorn for a star

when the world curls itself
around my fingers
10   seas gather in my palms
trees sustain the sky

      my life lifts to loving
      love leaps to living

      and without words i strive to answer
      questions you have never asked

oh making you understand
is like trying to crush
the skull of a mountain

KIZITO MUCHEMWA (1950–)

Tourists

They came into the wilderness clichés in suitcases
Talismans they cherished as shields against this poisonous madness
Lurking in the dark aggressive landscape of alienness.
Looking for recognition of this my dear land
They saw no familiar hills and heard no familiar songs.
Holding onto their fetishes they defy time and distance
Send lines across oceans to tap the energies
A faceless past economically nourishes wilting roots
Dying on the rocky exposures of understanding through fear.

10   They surround themselves with jacarandas and pines,
Build concrete walls around their homes,
I hope next time they will import snow, change
The seasons to humour their eccentric whims.

Already other trinkets hoot their mockery of our lives
Proclaiming the raucous assertiveness of their makers
But this land, this; the spirits dwelling in it
Will not yield to such casual intimidation
Neither will it give out its rich sad secrets
To half-hearted tokens of transparent love.

CHRISTOPHER VAN WYK (1957–   )

Beware of White Ladies When Spring Is Here

Beware of white ladies
in chemise dresses
and pretty sandals
that show their toes.
Beware of these ladies
when spring is here.
They have strange habits
of infesting our townships
with seeds of:
10   geraniums pansies poppies carnations.
They plant their seeds in our eroded slums
cultivating charity in our eroded hearts
making our slums look like floral Utopias.
Beware!
Beware of seeds and plants.
They take up your oxygen
and they take up your time
and let you wait for blossoms
and let you pray for rain
20   and you forget about equality
and blooming liberation
and that you too deserve chemise dresses
and pretty sandals that show your toes.
Beware of white ladies
when spring is here
for they want to make of you
a xerophyte.

NOTES

PRAISES OF MASELLANE

Masellane ruled in the eighteenth century. Under him the tribe moved to the Pilansberg district of the western Transvaal. This fragment of his praises refers to his appropriating for his own cattle the earmark (a slit extending half-way down from the tip) used by a subject community, the Mabodisa. This action earned him the nick-name 'lord of the vulva.'

2 (literally) from the times of the ancestor gods.

5 a reference to his depriving the Mabodisa of their earmark.

PRAISES OF SHAKA

1 Dlungwana: praise-name, 'the rager' or 'the ferocious one.'

2 Mbelebele: Mbelebeleni was a military kraal.

5 Menzi: 'the Creator', a praise-name for Senzangakhona.

6 'He who beats': Nodumehlezi, Shaka's famous praise-name (water can be beaten but to no effect; Shaka cannot be beaten at all).

8 'I fear to say': it is unusual to mention a chief by name.

12 'the madman': a story that the young Shaka confronted and killed a madman who was terrorising the district.

17 Noju: one of Zwide's counsellors who conspired with Shaka.
Ngqengenye: one of Shaka's generals.

18 Ntombazi: Zwide's mother.
Nandi: Shaka's mother.

19 & 20 the red one of Ntombazi (Zwide) was lured by the white one of Nandi (Shaka) into Zululand where he was finally defeated.

OLD ENGLISH RIDDLES

a) The accepted solution is, Bookworm.

b) The accepted solution is, Fire (the 'two dumb creatures' must be flints, or even possibly pieces of wood).

c) The accepted solution is, Ice.

THE DEMON LOVER

This ballad exists in over 145 known versions. In many of them the woman has married a ship's carpenter, having forsaken her seaman lover.

THE SINGING MAID

As the refrain begins this lyric, and is repeated after each stanza, it is a carol — a dance song. Carols were not especially associated with Christmas until the fifteenth century and later.

I HAVE A GENTLE COCK

An echo of this lyric may survive in the nursery rhyme 'Goosey, goosey gander.'

ADAM LAY IBOUNDEN

'Adam' also represents humankind. Medieval Christian teaching was that after the fall humankind was subject to the 'bond' of Satan — to sin and death. According to one tradition, the Creation era was about 4 000 BC.

The *felix culpa* (the happy fruit) of Adam and Eve was celebrated at Easter. The forbidden fruit was identified with the apple in the fourth century, thereby giving rise to the useful Latin pun on *malum* (evil; apple).

(CHAUNTECLEER)
7 & 10 In the old astronomy, the equinoctal circle (a circle of the heavens in the plane of the earth's equator) made a complete revolution each day. This meant that fifteen degrees would pass, and ascend, every hour. Chauntecleer could measure this movement exactly and crow accordingly.

THE COMPLAINT OF CHAUCER TO HIS PURSE
The date of this poem is generally accepted to be between 30 September 1399, when Henry was received as king by parliament and 3 October, when Chaucer received a royal grant of an additional stipend. The invocation of Brutus, the descendant of Aeneas who, traditionally, had founded Britain, is thus important in Chaucer's supplication to the new king.

TO MISTRESS MARGARET HUSSEY
22 Isaphill: Hypsipyle (a legendary queen of Lemnos, renowned for her beauty and devotion to her family).
25 Cassander: Cassandra, the Trojan princess who prophesied the fall of Troy (she stands here for constancy).

THEY FLEE FROM ME
This poem exists in both manuscript, as given here, and in a form slightly rewritten by Richard Tottel, in his *Miscellany* (1557), with the rough, experimental metre normalised into regular iambic pentameter, and a more rhetorically pointed ending.
8 otherwise: at other times.
10 after a pleasant guise: in a merry way.
12 small: slender.
16 gentleness: nobility of heart.
19 newfangleness: fashionable, changeableness.

WHOSO LIST TO HUNT
1 list: wishes.
3 vain: futile.
   travail: effort.

I FIND NO PEACE
5 that: that which (love).
7 devise: plan.

TICHBORNE'S ELEGY
14 shade: shadow.
17 glass: hourglass.

THE SILVER SWAN . . .
1 had no Note: did not sing.

WEEP YOU NO MORE SAD FOUNTAINS
4 waste: wear away.

AS YOU CAME FROM THE HOLY LAND
18 as unknown: as if she didn't know me.
32 fast: fixed.
33 dureless: ever-enduring, without end.
    content: happiness.
34 trustless: not to be trusted in.
36: toy: trifle.
40 conceits: imaginings.
45 durable: lasting.

ON THE LIFE OF MAN
2 division: conflict, but also a musical term for a rapid melodic passage.
3 tiring-houses: dressing rooms.
9 latest: final.

MORE THAN MOST FAIR ...
9 frame: construct.

ONE DAY I WROTE HER NAME ...
4 pains: effort.
5 assay: attempt.
8 eek: also.

WITH HOW SAD STEPS ...
10 wit: intelligence.

OFT HAVE I MUSED ...
14 annoy: mortal discomfort.

THEY THAT HAVE POWER ...
6 husband: manage with thrift and prudence.

WHEN MY LOVE SWEARS ...
1 truth: fidelity (as well as verbal truthfulness).
5 vainly: illusorily.
7 simply: as a simpleton might.
9 unjust: unfaithful.
11 habit: dress, clothing.
12 told: counted (as well as spoken).
13 lie with: make love to (as well as 'speak untruths').

NOT MARBLE, NOR THE GILDED MONUMENT
13 that yourself arise: when you yourself will arise.

LITANY IN TIME OF PLAGUE
10 physic: medical skill.
19 Helen: Helen of Troy, legendary beauty.
23 Hector: legendary hero of the Trojan wars.
36 degree: social class.

SWEETEST LOVE, I DO NOT GO

11 sense: capacity for perception.

A VALEDICTION: FORBIDDING MOURNING

11 spheres: non-material spheres were thought by old astronomers to revolve around the earth.
12 innocent: not harmful.
14 sense: limited to physical sensation.

STILL TO BE NEAT, STILL TO BE DRESSED

2 As: as if.

EPISTLE: TO MY LADY COVELL

(title) — Lady Covell: well known as patron of the arts.
11 twenty stone: over 125 kg.
13 Marry: indeed.
17 jealousy: anxious concern.
18 by: in attendance.
24 Joan: name for a female servant.

ON MY FIRST SON

1 Benjamin, the Hebrew name, means 'of my right hand', i.e., favourite.
10 Ben Jonson his: Ben Jonson's.
poetry: the word derives from the Greek word for 'poet', which means 'maker' (of verses).

ON SPIES

2 snuff: candle end.

DELIGHT IN DISORDER

2 kindles . . . a wantonness: has a provocative effect.
3 lawn: fine linen.
4 distraction: state of disarray.
6 stomacher: a garment covering the breast.

DENIAL

10 alarms: sudden attacks.

VIRTUE

10 sweets: delights.
11 closes: endings.

(SATAN)

7 Nine times: in Greek myth, the Titans, overthrown by Zeus, fell nine days and nights from heaven to earth and nine more down to Tartarus, a dark region beneath the earth.
14 witnessed: reflected, expressed.
16 angels ken: either 'angels' apprehension' or 'angels apprehend'. Satan still has an angel's range of vision.
20 No light: in theological tradition the fires of hell gave forth no light.
visible: that can be seen through.
29 utter: outer.

31 'thrice' is indefinite, not an exact measurement.
45 The mind is its own place: for Milton heaven and hell were states of mind as well as places.
48 all but: scarcely.

WHEN I CONSIDER HOW MY LIGHT IS SPENT
13 post: travel.

OUT UPON IT!
3 like: likely.

TO HIS COY MISTRESS
7 Humber: the river on which Hull, the town where the poet lived, is built.
40 in his slow-chapt power: in the power of his slow-moving jaws.

BERMUDAS
9 wracks: wrecks (verb).
12 prelate: dignitary of the Catholic and Anglican churches.
14 enamels: brightly decorates.
20 Ormus: an ancient Persian city.
23 apples: exotic pineapples.
36 Mexique Bay: the Gulf of Mexico.

THE RETREAT
18 several: separate.
    sense: faculty of perception or sensation.

A DESCRIPTION OF THE MORNING
10 kennel edge: edge of the gutter.
14 Moll is selling brickdust, used as an abrasive for cleaning.

EPISTLE TO MISS BLOUNT . . .
    (title) — coronation: of George I.
4 spark: a fashionably elegant young man. Also figurative.
7 Zephalinda: Pope invents classical names for Miss Blount. See also line 46.
11 plain-work: plain as opposed to fancy needlework.
13 park: Saint James's Park or Hyde Park, places of fashionable resort.
    assembly: public social gathering.
24 whisk: whist.
    toast in sack: piece of toast in white wine.
38 flirt: sudden movement of the fan.
43 crew: crowd.
47 Gay: John Gay, a friend of Pope's, and fellow poet.
48 chairs: sedan-chairs.

ODE, ON THE DEATH OF A FAVOURITE CAT
3 blow: bloom.

SONGS OF INNOCENCE AND EXPERIENCE
The first 'Nurse's Song' printed here is from *Songs of Innocence*; the remainder of the poems are from *Songs of Experience*.

FOR A' THAT AND A' THAT
8   gowd: gold.
10 hoddin: coarse cloth.
17 birkie: fellow.
20 coof: brainless person, fool.
28 fa': attempt.
36 gree: prize, victory.

STRANGE FITS OF PASSION HAVE I KNOWN
15 cot: cottage.

LINES COMPOSED A FEW MILES ABOVE TINTERN ABBEY . . .
113 genial: inborn, native.

FROST AT MIDNIGHT
15 'In all parts of the kingdom these films (of soot) are called *strangers* and are supposed to portend the arrival of some absent friend.' (Coleridge)
24 Christ's Hospital School which Coleridge entered at the age of nine.
28 birth-place: the country town of Ottery Saint Mary in Devonshire.
52 cloisters: of his school.

KUBLA KHAN
1   Kublai Khan, 12.16.1294, a grandson of Genghis Khan and emperor of China. Coleridge knew the following description in *Purchas His Pilgrimage* (Samuel Purchas, 1613): 'In Xanadu did Kublai Khan build a stately Palace, encompassing sixteen miles of plaine ground with a wall, wherein are fertile Meddowes, pleasant springs, delightful streames, and all sorts of beasts of chase and game, and in the middest therof a sumptuous house of pleasure.'
3   River Alph: from 'Alpha,' first letter of the Greek alphabet.
41 Mount Abora: possibly Coleridge had in mind the following lines from Milton's *Paradise Lost*: 'where *Abassin* Kings their issue Guard,/Mount *Amara*, though this by some supposed/True Paradise under the Ethiop line' (IV, lines 280—82).

SONNET ON CHILLON
(title) — Chillon: castle on an island in Lake Geneva.
13 Bonnivard: a Genevese who was imprisoned by the Duke of Savoy in Chillon for his courageous defence of his country against the tyranny with which Piedmont threatened it during the first half of the seventeenth century.

from: BEPPO
6   Habeas Corpus: order requiring person to be brought before a judge or into court, especially to investigate the right of the law to keep him in prison.
15 Regent: George, Prince of Wales, who acted as Regent owing to the insanity of his father, George III.
18 Poor's Rate: a rate or assessment for the relief or support of the poor, felt to be a financial burden by wealthier members of the population.

20 *Gazette: The London Gazette*, which was a record of official appointments, notices of bankruptcies, etc.

24 Tories: name of one of the two main political parties in England which, from the time of George III, upheld the constituted authority and order in church and state.

ENGLAND IN 1819

1 King: George III who died the following year (1820).

7 stabbed . . . field: the Manchester or Peterloo Massacre. On 16 August 1819, a mass meeting of unarmed workers in Saint Peter's Field, Manchester, was dispersed by cavalry troops which had been rashly summoned in panic by the magistrates. Eleven people were killed and over four hundred injured.

10 Golden and sanguine: paid for by gold and carried out with violence.

12 Time's worst statute: the law which barred Roman Catholics and Dissenters from holding office.

ODE TO THE WEST WIND

This poem should be read in the context of the revolutionary climate of Europe at the time.

BRIGHT STAR

4 Eremite: hermit (usually with a religious connotation).

WHEN I HAVE FEARS . . .

3 charactery: handwriting or printing.

TO AUTUMN

28 sallows: willows.

30 bourn: region.

32 croft: fenced plot.

AFAR IN THE DESERT

Poem based on the experience of Pringle's ride from Somerset to Cape Town in 1822.

13 Native Land: Scotland.
Pringle arrived in the Eastern Cape with a party of 1820 Settlers and remained in South Africa for six years, during which time he wrote his 'South African' poems.

48 grey forests: 'It grew in a secluded glen or *kloof*, running up the subsidiary ridges abutting from the Zureberg.' (Pringle, *African Sketches*).

69 Wilderness vast: the Kalahari, north of the Orange River.

71 Coránna: a tribe of the Khoi which inhabited the banks of the Gariep (Orange River).

92 Elijah: fortified against despair and isolation on Mount Horeb by God's 'still small voice,' he was reminded of the value of good work among men, even in an imperfect world. (O.T.)

MAKANNA'S GATHERING

(title) — Makanna: (or Makhanda), early nineteenth-century warrior and self-proclaimed prophet of the amaXhosa, directed the council of the confederated Chiefs and, after invasion of his country by British troops in 1818, led an unsuccessful attack on the garrison in Graham's Town. Imprisoned on Robben Island, he drowned in 1819 while leading an escape of prisoners. Has near-legendary status in several protest works by contemporary writers, where Robben Island is known as the Isle of Makhanda.

10 sons of Káhabee: descendants and vassals of Káhabee, the patriarch of the amaXhosa tribes.
17 Uhlanga: Supreme Being; also the name of the oldest of the amaXhosa kings and by whose name the tribes swore in former days.
21 Amanglézi: plural of Englézi, one from England.
23 Umláo's feeble sons: Xhosa reference to those Khoikhoi who had been colonised.
43 wizard-wolves: superstition that wolves were employed by sorcerers to commit ravages of those they disliked; alternatively that sorcerers sometimes assumed the shape of wolves.

NATURE'S LOGIC
Written in Cape Town, 1825.

ULYSSES
Ulysses (Odysseus) is the hero of Homer's *Odyssey*, a work which records the fantastic adventures of the Greek warriors on their way home after the Trojan War. Ulysses eventually reached his island kingdom, Ithaca.

10 Hyades: stars which bring rain.
63 the Happy Isles: islands, situated beyond the Mediterranean, in which dwell the spirits of the dead.
64 Achilles: one of the Greek heroes killed in the Trojan War.

MY LAST DUCHESS
Ferrara: in 1564, Duke Alfonso of Ferrara, Italy, was negotiating his marriage to the niece of the Duke of Tyrol.

CAVALRY CROSSING A FORD
7 guidon: flag carried by cavalry troop.

DOVER BEACH
15 Sophocles: ancient Greek writer of tragedies.

THE WHEEL OF FORTUNE
21 'quantum suff' (sufficit): originally formula used in medical prescription (meaning as much as suffices).

EPITAPH ON A DIAMOND DIGGER
5 'wight': man; spotless white (diamond).

THERE CAME A WIND LIKE A BUGLE
7 moccasin: (North American) poisonous snake.

STELLENBOSH
(title): in the Boer War (1899–1902) the British base camp for military administration was at Stellenbosch.
21 Boojers: burghers, i.e. the Boers.
22 bandolier: cartridge-belt.

32 'elios: helios, heliographs; instruments for signalling by means of flashes of sunlight.
38 K.C.B.: a knighthood.
41 D.S.O.: a military decoration.

I KILLED A MAN AT GRASPAN
Australian troops served in the Imperial forces in the Boer War.
55 bandolier: cartridge-belt.

NO SECOND TROY
The woman who is referred to is Maud Gonne, with whom Yeats was in love for many years and who was involved, in a way of which he disapproved, in Ireland's struggle for freedom.
title — Troy: in Greek myth Helen's beauty led to her abduction and, in consequence, to the Trojan War.

EASTER 1916
A rising took place in Dublin at Easter in 1916 (during the First World War) against English rule. It was put down with great severity, and the leaders, described in the second stanza and named in the last, were executed. The effect of these executions was an increase in anti-English feeling.

ON A POLITICAL PRISONER
Con Markiewcz, imprisoned after her involvement in the Easter Rising (see 'Easter 1916', above).

DESIGN
2 heal-all: a medicinal plant.

XHOSA ROAD-MENDERS' CHANT
This poem attempts to re-create, in English, the rhythms and imagery of a traditional chant of the amaXhosa.

DULCE ET DECORUM EST
8 Five-Nines: shells containing poison gas.
This line was actually cancelled by Owen but its replacement — 'Of gas shells dropping softly that dropped behind' — might not have been finished.

MY SWEET OLD ETCETERA
2-3 recent war: Second World War.

EPIGRAMS
Holism: A term coined by General Smuts for his theory that the fundamental principle of the universe is the creation of wholes (the book *Holism and Evolution* was published by Smuts in 1926).
3 Bondleswaart: Namibian Khoi tribe whose refusal to pay dog tax in 1922 drew savage reprisals by the Smuts government.
4 Bull Hoek: a 'location' near Queenstown, C.P., where men of an Ethiopian church group were killed by police and soldiers in a 'removal' in 1921.

'CIVILISED' LABOUR POLICY
Policy of job reservation for white South Africans under the government of Prime Minister J.B.M. Hertzog, 1924—39.

ALL DAY LONG

  7 Sine: province of Senegal; Senghor's home district.

THE FALL OF ROME

  6 Fisc: British Revenue Department.

13 cerebrotonic: intellectually invigorating.

     Catos: Cato the Elder, Roman statesman who uttered the words, 'Carthage must be destroyed!'

     Cato the Younger, Roman Stoic philosopher.

THE MENDI

    (title): a troopship in which about 7 000 unarmed members of the S.A. Native Labour Contingent lost their lives when it sank after striking a mine in February 1917. This poem published 18 March 1939 in *Bantu World*.

MEMORIES OF WEST STREET AND LEPKE

  4 'hardly passionate Marlborough Street': Henry James said that an example of extreme understatement would be that Marlborough Street was hardly passionate.

14 C.O.: conscientious objector.

21 West Street Jail (in New York), from which prisoners were sent elsewhere.

26 Abramowitz: an inmate whom Lowell remembers as a slightly eccentric vegetarian and a pacifist.

42 Lepke: Lou (Lepke) Buchalter, one of the leaders of New York's labour and industrial racket, and a member of the ruling board of Murder Inc. went to electric chair in 1944.

MORAL STORY

  7 & 9 in Roman myth, heavenly Pair of twins, Castor and Pollux of the constellation Gemini; emblems of true love and constancy.

ONE NIGHT AT VICTORIA BEACH

    (title): Victoria Beach in Lagos.

  4 Aladuras: a Christian sect addicted to ritual bathing (from the Yoruba word *adura*, meaning 'prayer').

  8 highlife: popular Nigerian dance music.

25 Babalawo: a Yoruba traditional dinner.

PLAYBOY

  4 Archimedes: ancient Greek mathematician and inventor.

TO THE ETRUSCAN POETS

    (title) Etruscan: archaic culture which gave way to Roman conquest.

MR BLEANEY

  2 Bodies: motor car factory (slang).

17 four aways: section of British football-pool forms requiring competitors t predict four wins by teams playing away from their home-grounds.

HALF A WEEK AROUND THE NEW MOON

12 Mephisto: the Devil Mephistopheles.

A RIVER

1 Madurai: Indian city that has for about 2 000 years been the seat of Tamil culture and therefore traditional home of poets of the past and the present.

THEY SAY

4 our struggle: Matthews is a contemporary black South African writer.

THE ZOO AFFAIR

10 Tagore: Sir Rabindranath (1861-1941), great Indian poet.

COME THUNDER

Okigbo died in the cause of Biafran succession in the Nigerian civil war (1967–70).

TO THE PUPILS OF NATHANIEL NYALUSA HIGH SCHOOL . . .

Manisi is an *imbongi*, a traditional oral poet of the Xhosa-speaking people, who today performs his poetry wearing the *imbongi*'s traditional cloak and hat of animal skin and brandishing two spears. The last war fought by the Xhosa against white settlers ended in 1878. In changed social circumstances, Manisi exploits the tradition in which he operates, one involving praise, criticism and heroic inspiration, in order to compose this poem spontaneously, in performance, and without premeditation. (See Pringle's 'Makanna's Gathering').

3 Literally, those who wear skirts.

4 Literally, those who lay petty accusations, referring to charges laid by the white settlers on the frontier against the Xhosa for raiding cattle, a traditional pursuit.

5 Nonibe, wife of the Xhosa chief Ngqika (c. 1780–1829), was assigned responsibility for the whites settled on Xhosa land.

9 *iGqum' eliselwandle*, 'it roars in the sea,' is an old Xhosa name for Algoa Bay, where parties of the British settlers landed in 1820. Rharhabe was the grandfather of Ngqika. The line of descent of the Xhosa chiefs is as follows: Xhosa . . . Tshiwo – Phalo – Rharhabe – Mlawu – Ngqika – Sandile . . . Mxolisi – Maxhobandile (still in his minority).

11 *iGqum' eliphezulu*, 'it roars on high,' is an old Xhosa name for the site occupied by Grahamstown, which became the major town of the new British settlers.

34 Ivory bands were worn on the upper arm by warriors of distinction.

58 Lennox Sebe is the Chief Minister of Ciskei, the 'homeland' established by the South African government for the Xhosa people.

58 Chief Lent Maqoma, acting paramount chief of the Xhosa, is Minister of the Interior of the Ciskei government and a direct descendant of the warrior-hero Maqomo (d. 1873), son of Ngqika.

59 Chief Sipho Burns-Ncamashe of the Gwali people was Minister of Education in the Ciskei government before he became leader of an opposition party.

4–6 Mngqesha is the current royal seat of the Xhosa paramount chiefs.

Maxhobandile, son of the late paramount chief Mxolisi, is a student in his minority, and will in due time succeed to the chieftainship.

MAYFAIR

(title): in southern Johannesburg.

THE CHILDREN OF NONTI

1 Nonti Nzimande: ancestral village elder (Zulu).

INDEX OF POETS

(*denotes South African poet)

ACKNOWLEDGEMENTS

The editors and publisher gratefully acknowledge the following copyright holders
for permission to use poems in this anthology:

Lionel Abrahams for his poems and one poem by Ruth Miller; W.H. Auden
'The Fall of Rome', reprinted by permission of Faber & Faber Ltd., from Collected
Poems by W.H. Auden; Shabbir Banoobhai for his poem; John Berryman: 'The
Ball Poem', reprinted by permission of Faber & Faber Ltd., from Homage to
Mistress Bradstreet by John Berryman; Guy Butler for his poems, and Ad. Donker
(Pty) Ltd.; Francisco Campbell Custodio and Ad. Donker (Pty) Ltd. for poems by
Roy Campbell; Jeremy Cronin for his poem; Patrick Cullinan for his poems; e.e.
cummings: 'my sweet old etcetera', 'ygUDuh', and 'Buffalo Bill's', from Complete
Poems 1913—1962 by e.e. cummings, reprinted with permission of Grafton Books
a Division of the Collins Publishing Group; T.S. Eliot: 'Rhapsody on a Windy
Night', reprinted by permission of Faber & Faber Ltd., from Collected Poems
1909—1962 by T.S. Eliot; The Hogarth Press and Watson, Little Ltd., for poem
by D.J. Enright; Robert Graves: 'The Cool Web' and 'Counting the Beats', reprinted
by permission of A.P. Watt Ltd., from The Collected Poems by Robert Graves
Thom Gunn: 'Elvis Presley', reprinted by permission of Faber & Faber Ltd., from
The Sense of Movement by Thom Gunn; Mafika Pascal Gwala for his poem and
Ad. Donker (Pty) Ltd.; Seamus Heaney: 'Follower', reprinted by permission of
Faber & Faber Ltd. from Death of a Nationalist by Seamus Heaney; Ted Hughes
'Snowdrop', 'The Thought-Fox', and 'Crow's First Lesson', reprinted by permission
of Faber & Faber Ltd.; Elizabeth Jennings: 'My Grandmother' and 'Ghosts', re-
printed by permission of David Higham Associates Ltd. from Collected Poems by
Elizabeth Jennings; Wopko Jensma for his poems; Rudyard Kipling: 'Stellenbosh'
reprinted by permission of The National Trust for Places of Historic Interest or
Natural Beauty and Macmillan London Ltd., from Stellenbosh by Rudyard Kipling
Philip Larkin: 'Mr Bleaney', reprinted by permission of Faber & Faber Ltd. from
The Whitsun Weddings by Philip Larkin and 'Next Please', reprinted by permission
of The Marvell Press from The Less Deceived by Philip Larkin; Douglas Livingstone
for his poems and Ad. Donker (Pty) Ltd.; Robert Lowell: 'Memories of West Street
and Lepke' reprinted by permission of Faber & Faber Ltd.; James Matthews for
his poem; Mbuyiseni Oswald Mtshali for his poem and Ad. Donker (Pty) Ltd.
K. Muchemwa: 'Tourists' and Charles Mungoshi: 'If you don't stay bitter and angry
for too long', reprinted by permission of Mambo Press from Zimbabwean Poetry
in English, 1978; Njabulo S. Ndebele for his poem; Gabriel Okara: 'One Night
Victoria Beach' and 'Piano and Drums', reprinted by permission of Heinemann
Educational Books Ltd. from The Fisherman's Invocation by Gabriel Okara
© Gabriel Okara 1978; Christopher Okigbo: 'Come Thunder', reprinted by permis-
sion of Heinemann Educational Books Ltd. from Labyrinths with Path of Thunder
by Christopher Okigbo, © Legal Personal Representative of Christopher Okigbo
1971; Sylvia Plath: 'Mushrooms' and 'Morning Song', published by Faber & Faber
Ltd., © Ted Hughes and reprinted by permission of Olwyn Hughes; William Plomer
'The Scorpion', reprinted by permission of the Estate of William Plomer and
Jonathan Cape Ltd. from Collected Poems by William Plomer; Ezra Pound: 'In a
Station of the Metro' and 'The River-Merchant's Wife: A Letter', reprinted by
permission of Faber & Faber Ltd., from Collected Shorter Poems by Ezra Pound
David Philip Publisher (Pty) Ltd. for permission to reprint 'Frog' by Sydney
Clouts, 'Mayfair' and 'Sunflower' by Stephen Gray, 'Naturalists' by Chris Mann

and 'Poem for my Mother' by Jennifer Davids; A.K. Ramanujan: 'A River', reprinted by permission of Oxford University Press from *The Striders and Other Poems*, 1966; John Crowe Ransom: 'Bells for John Whiteside's Daughter', reprinted by permission of Alfred A. Knopf/Random House, Inc. and Methuen London, Ltd. from *Selected Poems* by John Crowe Ransom; Léopold Sédar Senghor: 'All Day Long' reprinted by permission of Oxford University Press, from *Selected Poems of Léopold Sédar Senghor*, translated by John Reed and Clive Wake, 1964; Sipho Sepamla for his poem and Ad. Donker (Pty) Ltd.; Mongane Wally Serote for his poems and Ad. Donker (Pty) Ltd.; R.J. Slater for poems by Francis Carey Slater; Wallace Stevens: The Poems of our Climate' reprinted by permission of Faber & Faber Ltd. from *The Collected Poems of Wallace Stevens*; Peter Strauss for his poem; Vincent Swart: Casey Jones', reprinted by permission of Marcia Leveson from *Collected Poems* by Vincent Swart; Dylan Thomas: 'Fern Hill', reprinted by permission of David Higham Associates Ltd., from *Collected Poems* by Dylan Thomas; Anthony Thwaite: 'Called For', reprinted by permission of Anthony Thwaite and Martin Secker & Warburg Ltd. from *Poems 1953—83* by Anthony Thwaite; Charles Tomlinson: 'Paring the Apple', reprinted by permission of Oxford University Press from *Collected Poems*, 1985 by Charles Tomlinson; Christopher van Wyk for his poem and Ad. Donker (Pty) Ltd; Richard Wilbur: 'Playboy', 'Praise in Summer' and 'To the Etruscan Poets' by permission of Faber & Faber Ltd. from *Poems 1943—1956* by Richard Wilbur; William Carlos Williams: 'The Red Wheelbarrow' and 'The Lonely Street', reprinted by permission of New Directions from *Collected Earlier Poems* by William Carlos Williams, copyright 1938 by New Directions Publishing Corporation; David Wright for his poem and Ad. Donker (Pty) Ltd.; D.L.P. Yali-Manisi: 'To the Pupils of Nathaniel Nyalusa High School, Grahamstown 3 June 1979', reprinted by permission of the poet, and Jeff Opland, the translator; W.B. Yeats: 'No Second Troy', 'Easter 1916', 'On a Political Prisoner' and 'The Man and the Echo', reprinted by permission of Michael B. Yeats and Macmillan London Ltd., from *Collected Poems* by W.B. Yeats.

Although every effort has been made to trace the copyright holders, this has not always been possible. Should any infringement have occurred, the publisher apologises and undertakes to amend the omission in the event of a reprint.